PRAISE FOR
AWAKENING THE FIVE
CHAMPIONS:

"Living and working internationally, my family often transitions between cultures. *Awakening the Five Champions* equips my teenagers with the inner strength and adaptability they need to thrive. Its lessons on resilience and self-understanding are relevant for any young person, regardless of background."

DON KILBURG, PH.D., DIPLOMAT AND PARENT OF TEENAGERS

"Dr. Razzino, based on his experience, education, and good science, presents a readable and engaging book for both adults/parents and young emerging adults. Life is complicated but pending one's perspective is a change to grow to an impressive adult. In *Awakening the Five Champions,* Dr. Razzino gives the reader types of persons one may choose to become both the adaptive and the maladaptive. Moreover, he provides in each chapter functional approaches on how to live and emerge as a stronger and successful adult. Good read, good information, good focus. This book is something you will enjoy."

DN. JOSEPH R. FERRARI, PH.D., PROFESSOR OF PSYCHOLOGY AND SAINT VINCENT DE PAUL DISTINGUISHED PROFESSOR, DEPAUL UNIVERSITY

"There are tools in this book for all teens and the adults who love and work with them. Dr. Razzino identifies the risks and opportunities that are a natural part of adolescence, as well as the specific challenges facing most young people today. He draws on both science and practical examples to create a framework to support healthy development and relationships, using appealing metaphors as natural shortcuts for both understanding and recollection. What's more, he lays out exercises to practice the skills in the framework to make them stick. This book is a great resource to help young people thrive."

MARY ANN MCCABE, PH.D., ABPP, CLINICAL PSYCHOLOGIST, BOARD-CERTIFIED IN CLINICAL CHILD AND ADOLESCENT PSYCHOLOGY

"*Awakening the Five Champions* should be a must read for both teens and their parents. Even with my twenty-five years of experience working with teens and their families, I learned from the book. It is clearly written, with actionable exercises for teens to challenge their thought patterns at a time when their brains are still very malleable. It is a great guide to help teens develop into emotionally healthy adults."

JOSHUA WEINER, M.D., BOARD-CERTIFIED ADULT AND CHILD/ADOLESCENT PSYCHIATRIST

AWAKENING
THE FIVE
CHAMPIONS

....

Keys to Success for Every Teen

BRIAN E. RAZZINO, PH.D.

Razzino and Associates
FALLS CHURCH, VIRGINIA

Razzino and Associates / Brian E. Razzino
Website: DrBrianRazzino.net

Cover design by Gus Yoo
Editing and book production by Stephanie Gunning

Awakening the Five Champions / Brian E. Razzino —1st edition

Library of Congress Control Number: 2024923139

ISBN 979-8-9917945-0-3 (paperback)
ISBN 979-8-9917945-1-0 (ebook)

To Robin, Zoe, and Anna,
with all of my heart.

CONTENTS

Preface *ix*

Introduction *xi*

CHAPTER 1

The Mastermind and *1*

the Dark Legion

CHAPTER 2

The Warrior *23*

CHAPTER 3

The Wizard *59*

CHAPTER 4

The Lover *91*

CHAPTER 5

The Healer *131*

CHAPTER 6

The Seeker *163*

Conclusion *201*

Acknowledgments *227*

Resources *229*

About the Author *231*

PREFACE

M y journey of becoming a psychologist started long before I knew what the word *psychologist* meant. Growing up in Chicago, life wasn't easy. My family struggled with poverty and addiction, and we went through some really tough times. These experiences shaped me deeply. Early on, I realized how powerful it is to have someone there for you when you're struggling, and I knew I wanted to be that person for others.

When my family went into therapy, it opened my eyes to the strength and resilience we all have inside, even when we don't realize it's there. That was the spark that set me on the path to where I am today.

With over twenty-five years of experience working with kids, teens, and families, I've made it my mission to help young people find sources of strength within themselves. Whether someone is dealing with anxiety and depression, or just figuring out how to navigate life's ups and downs, I'm passionate about being there for them during their toughest times.

From having faced my own challenges, I've learned that our struggles can fuel us to grow, learn, and help others along the way. When I'm not working with kids and families, I'm spending time with my wife and two daughters, who remind me every day why I do the work I do.

Awakening the Five Champions is my way of passing on what I've learned—from my own life and the many lives of those I've had the honor to support—so you can find the strength you need to face your challenges, be resilient, and live well and happily. That's my definition of success. You are not alone in your journey through the transition from adolescence to adulthood.

INTRODUCTION

O ver the years, I've learned that placing our experiences in a context by using metaphors and imagery to describe them makes them easier to understand and work with. For instance, the metaphor of being *lost at sea* can help you acknowledge how vulnerable uncertainty makes you feel, while comparing yourself to a *phoenix rising* may inspire you to be resilient after a failure or disappointment. But it's one thing to know whether you feel sad or uncertain, and another to understand that your emotions reflect where you are in your life—in your family dynamics, relationships, or personal journey—so that you can be strategic and feel confident about the decisions and action steps you will take next.

In *Awakening the Five Champions: Keys to Success for Every Teen*, the central metaphor emphasizes that you are your own hero—the one who stands up for yourself and guides you in the right direction. This book isn't just about naming unpleasant emotions like doubt or insecurity; it's about awakening powerful forces within you that can help you see the bigger picture in any situation and guide you in moving forward in life. I've used the word *awakening* in the title deliberately because the Five Champions—the Warrior, the Wizard, the Healer, the Lover, and the Seeker—are already within you. You're not *creating* them, you're *awakening* them. These forces of bravery, creativity, empathy, learning, and adventure are pieces of you, and once you develop them, you can fully access strengths you probably don't even know yet that you possess.

What This Book Can Do for You

Your teenage years are a time of transformation when you're being tasked with determining who you are and what you want out of life. You might feel overwhelmed by needing to make many decisions—everything from choosing your classes and whether or not to join a club to deciding whom to date or hang out with—and by needing to manage the pressures arising from schoolwork, participating in sports, or your exposure to social media.

But even if these years seem complex and fraught with difficulty, this is an ideal stage of your life for growth and discovery. As you learn to rise to the occasion, again and again, you'll realize just how much potential you hold within you and get comfortable with using your power.

Imagine the Five Champions as different aspects of your being that can and will help you overcome specific challenges of adolescence. For instance:

- **The Warrior** embodies bravery and resilience, so it can help you face and get through tough situations, like standing up to a bully at school or experiencing fear of failure in sports or academics.
- **The Wizard** represents creativity and innovation, so it can help you think outside the box and be brilliant when you're

working on a project, like coding a new app or writing a story.

- **The Healer** brings compassion and empathy, so it can show you how to care for yourself and others, such as when a friend is going through a rough time or you're feeling stressed by something going on in your family.

- **The Lover** teaches connection and appreciation of beauty, so it can encourage you to appreciate the people around you and the little joys in life, like dancing to your favorite music, creating art, or playing with your dog or cat.

- **The Seeker** inspires curiosity, so it can push you to explore new ideas and experiences, like diving into a new hobby, questioning what you've been taught, or discovering new perspectives through travel or learning. The Seeker pushes you to expand your boundaries and ideas about who you are, and encourages you to take chances in this exploration as well.

In *Awakening the Five Champions,* I'm going to teach you how to find and activate these different abilities. To be clear, the Five Champions aren't just quirks or preferences, like enjoying pineapple on your pizza or sleeping on your right side. They also aren't fixed traits, like being an introvert or extrovert. The Five Champions are profound natural capacities that every human being possesses.

Furthermore, when I talk about these aspects of your identity, I'm describing ways of thinking and acting that you can cultivate and apply as necessary to any situation you encounter for the rest of your life. Together, they'll offer you a blueprint for channeling your energy.

Where It All Started

When humanity was still in its infancy, in the Paleolithic era, early humans lived much like animals, hunting, foraging, and seeking shelter in caves. It was during this time, as our ancestors were adapting to the challenges of survival, that the extraordinary capacities I call the Five Champions emerged. These innate abilities got etched into the genetic code of our ancestors and began to shape the way humans thought, felt, and acted. Today, they're woven into the very fabric of your being. Among all sorts of other talents and traits, because of these superpowers, you are an inventive, creative problem solver and visionary thinker.

And because the Five Champions are present in the DNA of every cell in your body and brain, they're always ready to be awakened and given a purpose. Think of this book as a training guide for activating your brain and heart so you can perform heroically in every aspect of your daily life. In it, I intend to show you how to use these powerful inner resources to skillfully navigate your journey of becoming a successful adult with confidence and inspiration.

Allow me to reiterate: The Champions aren't abstract ideas. They represent very real strengths that will become better defined and more reliable as you explore them and practice expressing them. History is filled with examples of ordinary people unlocking extraordinary capabilities through their focus and intention. That's what is possible for you in the future.

These abilities are not random, but rooted in the architecture of the human brain. Within your brain and the brains of your friends are neural circuits that activate the "personality" of each of the Five Champions—patterns of thought, emotion, and behavior that are associated with bravery, creativity, compassion, love, and curiosity—and these mental circuits are biologically programmed to help you in specific ways. By training in the ways these circuits function, you can strengthen the traits of the Champions and make them an integral part of your everyday life. You can call on these keys to success any time you're facing the kinds of challenges teens often encounter, like navigating friendships, figuring out what you want for your future, or dealing with the pressure of school and your parents' expectations.

By drawing out the best from you, the Five Champions will also help you use your unique qualities to bring light, peace, and prosperity to the world. The Warrior, the Wizard, the Healer, the Lover, and the Seeker are always ready to advocate for and support the real you—your authentic self—whenever needed. By embracing the Champions, you are not just unlocking your potential for personal gain, you are also contributing to a better world. The Champions can guide you to live in alignment with your values, lifting up both yourself and humanity.

How's This Gonna Work?

In Chapter 1, I will explain how to be the Mastermind of your life. As the ultimate decider of your fate, you will be the person who decides and has responsibility for calling upon the Five Champions that live inside you to handle different assignments which you set for them.

In each subsequent chapter, I'll introduce you to one of the Five Champions and the benefits it brings. I'll also show you how opposing counterparts to this Champion may try to hold you back, and teach you practical ways to overcome this internal "enemy." Every Champion has its counterpart. The Warrior is opposed by the Spoiler. The Wizard by the Distractor. The Lover by the Splitter. The Healer by the Neglector. The Seeker by the Deceiver. Collectively, I call these counterparts the Dark Legion.

The book is packed with activities that will help you put your ideas into action. Through stories, exercises, and real-life examples, you'll discover practical ways to build the strength of your Five Champions. The end of every chapter provides a special training program. As a result of doing these exercises, you'll not only feel more confident in who you are and clear about intentions but also equipped to handle whatever life throws your way—like a true Champion.

By the end of your reading journey, you'll have awakened your Five Champions. You'll be more resilient, creative, and confident, and ready to take on life's challenges with strength and determination. These Champions will help you form deep connections, discover your passions, and stay true to yourself, even when things get tough. At the same time, you'll have learned to spot the tricks of the Dark Legion and stop them before they take hold. Thus, you'll be able to live a life of purpose, positivity, and perseverance—like the Champion you're meant to be.

When you align your brain with the pattern of one of the Five Champions, it's like putting on a superhero suit—charging up your special powers and preparing for action. Just like a classic superhero's suit enhances the hero's strengths and equips them for battle, syncing with the neural patterns of one of the Champions empowers you to face challenges with poise and skill. This will improve your chances of success in all sorts of endeavors.

The process of "suiting up" is not just a mental exercise; it will give you a profound sense of connection to something greater: a universal order of being. As your brain aligns with these patterns and you unlock your true potential, you will be living out the promise encoded into your very genes. This alignment allows you to become a force for positive change, tapping into the wisdom, bravery, love, creativity, and healing that have always guided humanity's progress.

So, are you ready to suit up?

CHAPTER ONE

....

THE MASTERMIND AND
THE DARK LEGION

The mind is like a powerful symphony orchestra, with each section playing its part in creating a harmonious life. You, in your conscious mind, are what I call the Mastermind. You are the conductor who is directing this complex group of instruments. As the Mastermind, you hold the baton, make choices, take actions, and plan for the future. Your brain's ability to coordinate its different regions determines how effectively you think, feel, and act. When you consciously decide to think and act differently, you are training your internal orchestra to craft new mental routines for you. This prompts new brain circuitry to grow, enabling you to transform your personal reality—and, ultimately, the world around you—through the actions you take.

Each of us is a product of both our genes and the environment around us. Our family, peers, neighborhood, culture, economic status, and place in history shape our thoughts, feelings, choices, and decisions. These are powerful factors that help determine our personal view of the world and ourselves. But as much as the environment that we grow up in shapes us, so too do we shape our environment.

Because you are a Mastermind, you hold tremendous power—especially, the power to comprehend all the things that go into making you who you are and the power to change your thoughts and behavior. You also have the power to influence and change people and things around you. After all, you are part of the context in which others live. Your voice is a voice of influence and your choices impact the events that unfold in your environment.

You could uplift people like a student named Sarah who regularly starts her day by smiling and greeting her classmates warmly. Her positive energy elevates the spirits of her peers, and they, in turn, become more positive and friendly toward other students they interact with throughout the day. Sarah's greetings produce a ripple effect of kindness that transforms the overall atmosphere of any classroom she's in, making it a more welcoming and supportive environment.

Consider how influential movements throughout history have often started with the actions of a few determined individuals. Think of the civil rights movement of the 1960s, in which individuals like Rosa Parks and Martin Luther King, Jr., stood against racial injustice in the United States, inspiring countless others to join the cause. Their courage and determination created a powerful force for change, altering the social landscape of the entire country. They and their colleagues were able to communicate their vision so effectively that they extended their reach and galvanized people from all walks of life to participate in the movement.

In different places and times in history, the primary concerns and preoccupations of society have varied, but the impact of individual people's actions remains constant. In the late nineteenth century and early twentieth century, women like Susan B. Anthony and Emmeline Pankhurst fought for women's suffrage, radically transforming gender roles and societal expectations. Today, individuals like Greta Thunberg are influencing global awareness and action on climate change, reflecting the urgent concerns of our current era.

The fact that one person can make a difference is often lost on people. Too often, feeling powerless against profound, far-reaching forces larger than us, it is easy to start to feel resigned and hopeless, as if we have to settle for the world as it is. But consider something small that makes a big difference, like a community garden initiative. If one person starts planting flowers and maintains a small garden in a neglected area of their neighborhood, over time their neighbors are likely to join in, together creating a beautiful and productive space that fosters community spirit and collaboration. A simple act of starting a garden can lead to stronger community bonds and a renewed sense of pride and ownership in a neighborhood. In some communities, gardeners raise vegetables to supply local food pantries that serve low-income families with food insecurity. You could participate!

Furthermore, reflect on the impact of technological innovations driven by individual visionaries. Tech pioneers Steve Jobs and Bill Gates, for example, revolutionized personal computing, transforming how people interact with technology and each other.

Their innovative ideas and relentless pursuit of their goals have shaped the modern world, proving that one person's vision can indeed make a significant difference. Imagine how different our world would be if these visionaries had not believed in their abilities or sensed the change they could effect. Without Jobs' belief in creating user-friendly, aesthetically pleasing technology, Apple might never have developed the iPhone, which has reshaped global communication and daily life. Without Gates' vision of for putting a computer on every desk and in every home, personal computing might not be as widespread and integral to our daily routines as it is today.

Jobs and Gates also excelled at rallying others to their causes, building teams of talented individuals who shared their visions and worked tirelessly to bring them to fruition. Their ability to inspire and mobilize others extended their reach and magnified their impact, leading to additional innovations that revolutionized industries and daily life. Imagine a world without the internet as we know it, without the seamless integration of technology into our lives, and without the global connectivity that enables instant communication and access to information. These technological advancements have transformed industries and also how we learn, work, and connect with others.

The influence of such visionaries demonstrates the profound impact one person can have on the world, underscoring the power each of us holds to make a difference, regardless of the specific concerns and preoccupations of our time and place. Each action we take, no matter how small, has the potential to influence people in our environment and inspire them to change, creating a lasting legacy.

As the Mastermind possessing your special set of capabilities and interests, you have the power to deliberately shape your destiny. By honing your skills and talents and embracing this role, you can unlock extraordinary capabilities within yourself. The chapters in this book will guide you on how to harness these powers, turning your mind into the ultimate tool for creating a fulfilling and empowered life.

However, as the Mastermind, you will face challenges. The Dark Legion—forces that manipulate, distort reality, and exploits vulnerabilities—seek to keep you in a state of inaction and despair. In today's online world, these forces are greatly amplified, extending into your everyday life and adversely affecting how you think, feel, and behave.

The Battle Within: The Mastermind vs. the Dark Legion

Did you know you have a theme song? The running commentary in the background of your mind has themes that influence how you perceive and respond to the world. Just like the melodies that play behind the action in TV shows and movies, setting the mood of romance, a chase scene, or danger, your personal theme song sets the mood for your thoughts and actions. Each function of your brain plays a different "note," merging into a background song that can be inspiring or deflating, soothing or angering.

Your personal narrative, the story you tell yourself about who you are and what you can achieve, is like the lyrics to your theme song. These lyrics, which repeat again and again, sounding like chatter in your head, shape your perspective and guide your actions. This ongoing "song" of negativity or positivity profoundly affects your daily experiences. For this reason, your mind needs direction from you to manage the tone of your internal narrative. The goal of conducting or masterminding the different voices within ideally is to maintain harmony and balance.

Often, we are most influenced by negative experiences, which tend to change the tone of our theme songs. So, if you grew up in poverty, your theme song might include positive lyrics about the resilience of overcoming challenges, but also negative lyrics about the stress and anxiety of financial instability. If you come from a family of divorce, your theme song's lyrics might capture the complexities of navigating relationships and the emotional pain of family separation. Negative experiences can shape your views on trust, commitment, and security.

Your theme song is important because it influences your perceptions of people, places, and events, and sets up your expectations about the future. If your song has been shaped by betrayal or loss, you might approach new relationships with caution or skepticism. Conversely, if your theme song has been shaped by moments of support and success, you might view new opportunities with optimism and confidence.

The Dark Legion hijacks healthy impulses wired into your nervous system to protect and preserve you. Instincts like caution and vigilance, for instance, are essential for survival. When the Dark Legion is in control, these healthy impulses are transformed into fear, paranoia, and self-sabotage. The Dark Legion causes you to see threats where there are none, doubt yourself, and withdraw from valuable opportunities in life. For each of the Five Champions, there is a member of the Dark Legion that stands in opposition to it.

What's incredibly interesting to me, as a psychologist, is how the outer world mirrors our own inner voices. For example, online social networks are a breeding ground for the type of falsehoods and deceptions propagated by the Dark Legion. Posts in our feeds constantly bombard us with images of global warming, wars, political infighting, school shootings, and the worst sides of human nature. If we often feel anxious and confused about the state of the world, trying to make sense of both real and artificial news, these posts do nothing to soothe our spirits or to allay our fears.

Online, we are exposed to our peers' fears and worries, conspiracy theories, and catastrophic thinking (expecting the worst), which are highly contagious emotionally. This leads to increased feelings of helplessness as we rehash and hyper-focus on all the terrible things happening internally. The Dark Legion loves hearing the sound of its voices amplified.

The Dark Legion's influence will try to reach into every aspect of your life, from how you perceive yourself to how you interact with others. Cyberbullying, misinformation, and online predators exploit the anonymity of the internet to manipulate and harm, potentially contributing to severe emotional distress for you and your friends. Misinformation and conspiracy theories lead people down paths of fear and confusion by altering their perceptions and beliefs. And constant connectivity exposes you to unexpected interactions with people, topics, and activities that may not be in your best interest and can be harmful.

The Online World and Your Reality

In today's digital age, young people live between two versions of reality: one based in the physical world and the other in the virtual world. In the physical world, you engage in what we scientists call *embodied interactions*—face-to-face communication with real-time feedback, including nonverbal cues like body language and tone of voice, contributing to a richer understanding of interactions and relationships. The three-dimensional physical world is governed by natural laws and humanmade laws to reinforce social structure and maintain peace. People live, work, and relate based on economic, moral, and ethical principles.

Cultural transmission, the process through which values, beliefs, and practices are passed down from one generation to another, heavily relies on embodied experience. For example, learning to cook a family recipe involves more than just reading instructions online; it requires watching someone else cook and tasting ingredients, and sometimes even feeling the texture of ingredients, as guided by a family member. This hands-on experience of cooking conveys not just the recipe itself, but also the cultural significance, the familial bonds, and the stories tied to it. Then the recipe has an emotional resonance, too.

Similarly, participating in family traditions or local community events allows teens like you to experience their cultural heritage in a way that is deeply personal and impactful. The act of joining in a family cookout, hearing stories from grandparents, or even playing traditional board games provides a visceral connection to their history and identity that digital experiences alone cannot replicate.

By comparison, the virtual world transmits a different kind of culture altogether. Here, communication is often text-based or mediated through digital avatars that can strip away the nuances of timing, vocal tone, and nonverbal cues. Instead, teens are learning to use emojis, recycle put-downs, and come up with witty comebacks to earn acceptance at the expense of others.

The virtual world fosters a culture of instant information sharing, global connectivity, and digital trends that can quickly influence and shape behaviors and beliefs. These trends change quickly, making it hard to gain a sense of direction since it can feel like the earth is often shifting beneath your feet.

Online culture is infused with trolling, bashing those with different opinions, and mocking those with life experiences or views that are considered unfashionable or out of step with current trends. While the virtual world allows for unprecedented access to information and global connectivity, it often lacks the depth of personal connection and the hands-on learning needed to truly appreciate the nuances of foreign cultures. For example, while a teen can learn about different ways of life through videos or social media, these mediums can't fully capture the essence of participating in a cultural ritual, where the sounds, smells, and communal spirit are essential.

Understanding the balance between these two realms—one embodied, one virtual—is crucial for effective cultural transmission. While the virtual world can enhance and supplement learning, it is through real-life experiences in the physical world that the richest and most profound aspects of culture are truly transmitted and appreciated. The online world offers a new, rapidly evolving culture characterized by digital interactions and experiences, which can coexist with traditional culture but should not replace the real-life, embodied, in-person experiences that connect you to your heritage and identity.

The virtual world is governed by algorithms, providing a fragmented and distorted understanding of reality. These algorithms maximize engagement by exploiting psychological triggers like the need for validation, fear of missing out (FOMO), and instant gratification. The virtual world is driven by financial incentives, making money for a few the overarching objective. What you see is curated for maximum impact on you and to push the psychological triggers you and your peers tend to respond to.

Core dynamics shaping the virtual world include:

- Content Curation. Algorithms curate content based on past behavior and preferences, creating a personalized but narrow view of the world.

- Social Validation. Social media platforms encourage users to seek validation through likes, comments, and shares, reinforcing a feedback loop that can be addictive and lead to anxiety and depression.

- Information Bubbles. Personalized news feeds and content recommendations lead to information bubbles, exposing users only to viewpoints that align with their own, fostering polarization and limiting critical engagement with different perspectives.

You can escape into this online world anytime, much like the teleportation devices in science fiction. The device most people own today, the smartphone, opens gateways to remote parts of this online universe and new dimensions of activity that seem like reality.

Most people your age and older (over 90 percent) have constant access to their smartphones. This means you can leave familiar people and places and transport yourself to a world with endless information and countless ways to connect with others anonymously in digital and impersonal ways. Sounds pretty awesome, right? Still, this constant connectivity exposes you to unexpected interactions with people, topics, and activities that may not be in your best interest and can be harmful.

The one-to-many nature of online interactions means that your statements can quickly reach a broad audience, amplifying their positive and negative implications. Relationships and group memberships in online environments are often disposable, allowing quick changes in social dynamics without lasting commitment. Negative statements made about you by anonymous people vying for recognition can linger, eroding your self-esteem and well-being.

Have you ever stopped to notice the types of comments that stick with you? Are they usually the positive ones? If you are like most, it is the negative ones that have the most lasting impact.

Overcoming the Dark Legion

When you are playing the Mastermind role in your life, you continually write your own story through your choices, behaviors, feelings, and thoughts. Each decision, action, and emotion shapes your narrative, defining who you are and who you will become. This ongoing process empowers you to create your future in any form you desire.

Typically about 70–90 percent of your thoughts each day are the same as those from the previous day. Much of what is on your mind today is a rehash of what was there yesterday. About 80 percent of these duplicate thoughts are negative, focusing on injustices, embarrassments, fears, rejections, and disappointments. These repetitive routines and thoughts shape your perceptions and understanding of reality.

Each of us lives in a self-created reality bubble, maintained through self-fulfilling behaviors and ideas. Your sense of personality, self, and identity becomes ingrained through these habitual routines and experiences. This ingrained way of thinking makes it hard to see yourself in any other way or to recognize different opportunities when they arise.

It can be challenging to envision things being different from what you have come to know, especially if your past experiences have been predominantly negative, and even more so when your experiences of the real-time, embodied world are limited, for then you don't have contrasting experiences to help you envision alternative ways of being.

For too many young people, their view of the world includes continual feelings of discouragement and disempowerment due to negative, ingrained ideas about the world. This outlook has tremendous implications for how you see your life, the experiences you have, and your ideas about what the future holds.

For instance, imagine you have a big science test coming up. If you keep telling yourself, "I'm going to fail this test," you might not study as hard, you might feel more anxious, and then you might perform poorly, fulfilling your own expectation. This is a *negative self-fulfilling prophecy.*

On the other hand, if you tell yourself, "I can do well on this test if I study and stay focused," you're more likely to put in the effort, stay calm, and ultimately perform better. This is a *positive self-fulfilling prophecy,* where your positive expectations lead to a more empowering reality.

All of this happens without you being fully aware of it. The unconscious nature of these habits can mean you are living in and being controlled by your past. While you can never fully escape the impact of your earlier experiences, there is a tremendous amount you can do to direct the course of your life.

The top two things you can do are to:

- Choose Your Reality. The future is not written yet; it does not exist. You have the power to choose the type of life you want and how you wish to engage with the world. Your brain is still growing, organizing, and perfecting itself. Throughout your life, your brain will continue to change from new experiences, forming new connections and getting rid of others. Since your brain is still changing in significant ways each day, right now is an ideal time to take control of your world and the direction of your life. By doing so, you will start the process of rewiring your brain to help you create those new realities you desire most.

- Rewrite Your Script. You have the power to alter previous learning simply by thinking about it and changing the kinds of experiences you have. As the Mastermind, you can create your own story, write your own script, and reinvent who you are. By questioning and rewriting the expectations, attitudes, and beliefs set in your past, you open new possibilities and realities. As the Mastermind, you can choose the life you want, instead of being stuck in one imposed on you.

In the following chapters, you will learn about your Five Champion sides and how, as the Mastermind, you can choose to override past conditioning by actively engaging in mental rehearsal, visualization, and practicing new behaviors. By consistently practicing these new ways of thinking, feeling, and behaving you can transform your brain and step into a new reality of your own design.

Here are just a few areas we will touch on in coming discussions.

- Social Media Influence. Imagine scrolling through your social media feed and constantly comparing yourself to the seemingly perfect lives of others. You might start to believe that you need to look a certain way, have certain things, or behave in specific ways to be happy and accepted. As the Mastermind, you can question these influences and choose to value your unique qualities and interests, creating a reality where you feel confident and authentic.

- Academic Pressure. Think about the pressure to excel in school, get high grades, and participate in numerous extracurricular activities. This pressure can create a belief that your worth is tied to your achievements. However, if you step back and examine this belief, you might realize that it's shaped by external expectations. You can decide to redefine success for yourself, focusing on personal growth, creativity, and well-being rather than just on academic performance.

- Peer Dynamics. Consider the dynamics of your friend group. Maybe you've always played a specific role, like the "peacemaker" or the "funny one," because that's what others expect from you. By recognizing this pattern, you can choose to express different aspects of yourself, and befriend people who appreciate more of the qualities you have.

- Future Plans. Reflect on the expectations others have for your future, such as pursuing a particular career or lifestyle. These expectations might feel like the only path available, but they are based on someone else's vision for you. By exploring your own passions and interests, you can envision a future that excites and fulfills you, regardless of others' expectations.

- Identity and Personal Style. Think about how you dress and present yourself. Your choices might be heavily influenced by trends, peer pressure, or societal standards. But what if you experimented with styles that truly reflect your personality and creativity? By doing so, you can break free from external influences and develop a sense of identity that is genuinely your own.

As we touch on each of these areas, you, as the Mastermind, will learn to recognize and question external influences over your life. By doing so, you can create a reality that aligns with your true self, empowering you to be authentic while unleashing personal growth.

Now is a great time to learn these skills! As a teen, your brain is in the middle of a huge growth spurt, a critical developmental period, spurring new ways of thinking and feeling. This is a time in your life when you can more easily adopt new ideas and perspectives than you will be able to at any other time. It is also a time when you may question traditional ways of doing things, and your heart and soul yearn to be expressed through new ways of thinking and behaving.

Great Expectations

Young people like you face a ton of expectations in today's world. You're supposed to know all about tech and global issues, and to support causes like "Me Too" and "Black Lives Matter." It's a lot to handle. Plus you've got to keep up with trends, do well in school, care about the environment, and figure out your own identity and beliefs. All this plays out on social media, where everyone sees your wins and your struggles.

It's overwhelming, so it's no surprise that many teens feel stressed out. Anxiety and depression are rising, and it's hard to pinpoint just one reason why. Maybe it's all the screen time, worries about the planet, politics, or just the pressure to fit in and be perfect.

So, how do you figure out what you versus what others expect from you? You've been in a set routine for years: school, activities, homework, repeat. It's tough to break out and think for yourself. But eventually, you've got to make your own choices about what you want in life.

As you've grown from a young child to now, your way of thinking and understanding the world has changed dramatically. Part of this growth involves making more decisions for yourself and taking charge of what's important to you. Thinking for yourself is crucial, but it can also feel overwhelming. You may have become accustomed to people telling you what to do and when. However, as you've gotten older, you've realized that you want to be more in control of your own decisions. You have a mind of your own, and you want to use it to its fullest potential.

Making Up Your Mind

Knowing your own mind and how to make it work for you to its fullest will help you make more satisfying choices and claim purpose and direction in your life. When you are faced with the question, "What's the purpose of life?" —a question we all face— you can discover the answers for yourself. The purpose of your life can be whatever you want it to be. Each step is actually a decision, if you think about it, a decision only you have the power to make.

In this book, I will argue that life is about more than just the usual stuff, like finishing school, making friends, finding someone special, getting a job, buying things, or spending time online. It is likely you feel the same way, as you probably wouldn't be reading this book otherwise. Your life is way more (or at least it could be) than competing with others and buying fun toys and fancy clothes. While these goals consume the lives of many people, your life is much more than struggling, surviving, and climbing the social ladder.

Sure, part of your journey will involve having fun, messing around, goofing off, and partying with friends. This all contributes to discovering the joy, excitement, and wonder of life. But as you might have guessed, it's more than just that. Those moments of pleasure and excitement are crucial pieces of the puzzle, part of a larger process we might call *actualization.*

To visualize the process of actualization, imagine a seed growing into a mighty tree. Initially, the seed, nestled in the soil, seems insignificant. However, over time, it sprouts, develops roots, and eventually emerges from the ground. As years pass, it transforms into a strong, towering tree, unrecognizable from its humble origins. This tree then provides shelter, bears fruit, and becomes a vital part of the world and ecosystem.

The growth of this tree parallels your own development in our society. Just as the tree grows and is influenced by its environment—providing shelter and sustenance, influencing, and being influenced by other elements of its ecosystem—so do you in your social world. You started as an individual with potential, and through experience, you grew into the person you are today. However, you are more than just a composite of your experiences. You are a dynamic being who continuously shapes and is shaped by your surroundings, creating a unique whole that is greater than the sum of its parts.

Your process of growth continues until the end of your life. Born with certain tendencies that may limit and excite you, these traits contain the seeds of growth. This growth emerges from the stresses and struggles you experience each day, much like an oyster turning a grain of sand into a pearl. For instance, dealing with a difficult class in school can be frustrating, but it pushes you to develop better study habits and time management skills. Similarly, navigating social dynamics, like handling peer pressure or conflicts with friends, can be challenging but ultimately helps you build stronger relationships and resilience. The inherent challenges of being alive and human are not just obstacles but catalysts, pushing you to grow and evolve beyond the limits of your way of being.

Don't get me wrong, growth isn't only about serious stuff. It's also about enjoying all the fun and exciting things life has to offer. Having a good time, trying new things, and living in the moment are huge parts of why you're here. You grow and learn through all your experiences, and that includes making the most of life and the world around you, whether you're here for seventy, eighty, or even a hundred years.

Life isn't something just to try and survive. It can also be more than overcoming rough patches or accumulating wealth, fame, and property. Life can be a time of learning, making a difference, healing, and caring for others. You have the capacity to understand the world and its people on a much deeper level than you might know. Your journey of growing up will be filled with experiences that astonish, provoke, and inspire. Every challenge you face, every frustrating situation, is a piece of the puzzle, contributing to building an incredible, fulfilling life.

In the chapters that follow, we'll examine some of the most profound questions and challenges you face as a young person today. Throughout our discussions, the focus will remain on the most powerful component of change: you. On our journey, we will look at how you think about success, what you feel is most important, and the places, activities, and people that make you feel the most alive and whole. This means taking a hard look at the ever-present societal norms that often try to dictate what success is "supposed" to be and the pressures to conform to these standards. You will be encouraged to pursue trophies like marriage, high-status careers, wealth, homeownership, fame, and other material possessions as indicators of a fulfilling life and personal worth.

Final Thoughts about the Mastermind

The Dark Legion's influence is pervasive, but as the Mastermind you have the power to counteract these forces that exist within you. By engaging in real-world activities, practicing mindfulness, developing critical thinking, and consciously shaping the tone of the "background music" of your internal narrative, you can begin to create a reality that aligns with your true self.

Life is about more than simple survival. Yours can be full of meaning and purpose that brings you happiness and connection. Remember, you have the ability to choose and create a life you want.

The stage of life you're in, where you are transitioning from adolescence to adulthood, has unique challenges. But it is about thriving, growing, and becoming the person you are meant to be, like all other stages of life are, too, in their own ways. That is the human adventure.

As you navigate the challenges and opportunities of the digital world, remember: You hold the baton. You are the conductor of your life's symphony orchestra, and with intentionality and purpose, you can create a harmonious and fulfilling existence.

CHAPTER TWO

....

THE WARRIOR

Jenna is a fifteen-year-old high school sophomore trying to balance academics, extracurricular activities, and time with her friends. She's a dedicated dancer, enjoys painting, and has a close-knit group of friends, some from her elementary school days and others she met more recently. Jenna's parents describe her as a bright and creative teenager, but they've noticed fluctuations in her mood and behavior over the past year.

As a teenager, Jenna is discovering a range of new skills, abilities, and possibilities. Her brain is rapidly developing, forming new connections, and improving her judgment and decision-making abilities. This mental growth enables Jenna to think more critically and abstractly, allowing her to tackle complex problems and make more informed choices. Jenna is starting to see the world differently, noticing more than just what's right in front of her. She is becoming more aware of broader societal issues, future possibilities, and her own place in the world.

At the same time as Jenna's brain is changing, her body is undergoing significant changes, too. She's noticing her figure becoming more defined, her coordination improving, and her stamina increasing, which enhances her physical capabilities and self-confidence. Jenna is also experiencing new feelings of attraction and has curiosity about dating. She's started to notice boys differently and has had a few crushes, leading to both excitement and confusion.

Her new abilities create a mix of excitement and anxiety for Jenna. On one hand, the newfound mental and physical strengths fill her with enthusiasm and a sense of empowerment. She feels capable of achieving great things, whether it's perfecting a complex dance routine, creating captivating artwork, or engaging in meaningful social interactions. This excitement drives her to explore her potential, set ambitious goals, and seek out new opportunities.

On the other hand, the same abilities also bring about significant anxiety. The pressure to meet high expectations, whether self-imposed or from external sources like parents and teachers, can be overwhelming. Jenna often finds herself worrying about her performance in various areas, fearing failure or inadequacy. Her heightened awareness of social dynamics and future uncertainties can lead to self-doubt and stress. The contrasting messages she encounters on social media and the internet further complicate her emotional landscape, as she grapples with feelings of inadequacy compared to the seemingly perfect lives of others.

And then there's the whole drama of teenage relationships and trying to sort out her feelings about boys. That just adds another level of stress and excitement on top of everything else.

Jack is a thirteen-year-old middle schooler who is trying to balance academics, extracurricular activities, and time spent with his friends, just like Jenna. He's a passionate soccer player, enjoys playing the guitar, and has a close-knit group of friends, some from elementary school and others he met more recently. Jack's parents describe him as active, kind, and sensitive, but they've noticed him becoming more irritable, unfocused, and withdrawn lately.

Jack has noticed that he has the need to shower more often, and that his moods can sometimes be unpredictable, shifting between happy and carefree to worried and down. Meanwhile, his body is undergoing significant changes. He's noticing his muscles growing stronger and more defined, his voice deepening, and his overall physical strength increasing, which enhances his physical capabilities and self-confidence.

He's also started to notice the inconsistency between what the adults tell him is the right way to do things and how many of them actually behave themselves. At times, he's frustrated with the seemingly random rules and limits imposed on his freedom, like not being able to have his phone in his room after 8 PM, limits on his video gaming over the weekends, and new chores that he is now responsible for around the house like mowing the lawn and emptying the trash. Like Jenna, Jack is also starting to experience new feelings of attraction and has curiosity about dating. He's beginning to notice girls differently and has felt nervous excitement around certain classmates, which adds both thrill and confusion to his daily life.

Jack's brain is rapidly developing, leading him to find more to argue about with his parents, and he effectively makes his points about why he should be given some privileges. Jack is able to stay home alone for longer periods of time and is now looked on as the "responsible one," as compared to his younger siblings—a role that has both upsides and downsides. His parents recognize Jack's growing ability to think more critically and use good judgment, which gives them confidence to allow him to go on longer trips to the beach with his friend's family over the summer and help out at the local food kitchen with their church.

Jack is starting to see the world differently, noticing more than just what's right in front of him. He is becoming more aware of broader societal issues, future possibilities, and his own place in the world. And like Jenna, Jack finds people responding to him differently compared to his younger years. They talk to him more as an equal, ask his opinion on some important matters, and ask for his help fixing things and to pitch in to help elderly neighbors when they need it. While much of this is new, and it feels good, Jack has mixed feelings about it. He wonders if others see him accurately, if they expect too much from him, and if he is going to have enough time for fun and relaxation. He thinks a lot about what the future could look like once he is on his own. He wants to drive, get his own place, go to college, and find a career that makes him happy.

At times, Jack wants to go back to his old life of watching cartoons on Saturday mornings while eating his cereal and letting his parents pick out clothes for him during the school year. As much as he wants to make more decisions for himself, there seem to be so many of them to make. A lot of them he isn't sure he knows enough to make with confidence. It can be exhausting and overwhelming trying to figure everything out. Yet, he is reluctant to ask for help or admit he is confused for fear it will brand him as immature, unready, and incapable. He fears this will lead to more restrictions on his freedom, others to be critical of him, and accusations of "acting like a dumb kid."

Balancing the excitement of new possibilities with the anxiety of increased expectation is a central challenge for many young people like Jack and Jenna. As they navigate this period of change, they must learn to manage their internal dialogue, develop resilience, and figure out who to listen to and what examples to follow.

It is natural for you to want to use a new ability you discover. Like a new toy, you feel eager to explore its potential, experiment with it in different ways, and show it off to others. It's not much different from how, as little kid, when you could sit up, crawl, walk, talk, dance, climb, throw, and sing, you did so with boundless energy and joy, eager to test your limits and share your newfound skills with the world around you. This is true for everyone, and perhaps most especially teenagers and young adults. The excitement of mastering a skill while opening up novel dimensions of experience fills you with enthusiasm and a sense of accomplishment. In some cases, it may seem like you've found the keys to freedom and self-expression.

The part of you that is doing all this testing, figuring, and planning is the part I call the Warrior. This is a part of you that has great personal power and a strong sense of self. It is the part unafraid to ask for, or to pursue, what you want. It is a source of strength, courage, and the ability to act on the spot.

Freedom, or self-determination, is no small matter. Toddlers learn to say no soon after they begin speaking because they want to do things themselves, including choosing what that thing is going to be. "I can do it" is a favorite motto of the wee ones. It's as if when we are young, there is this force deep inside us that compels us to put the pedal to the metal, so to speak, and say, "See what this baby can really do!" If what we're doing was a new car that we were taking for a test drive, we'd want to know: How does it handle turns? Can it quickly get off the start or brake on a dime? Children may be too young to drive, but their enthusiasm for exploring the world through their bodies is remarkably similar. No matter our ages, our bodies are vehicles with which we may experience life.

An important rule of growing up is this: Because your body and brain are changing constantly, we can predict that your interests and activities will change constantly, too.

As Jack and Jenna move through their teenage years, their desire to explore their capabilities and push the boundaries of experience will remain strong. They're eager to test the limits of their expanding mental and physical skills, whether it's about Jenna perfecting a dance routine or Jack mastering a new soccer move. This phase in life is all about discovering what they can do and understanding their growing independence and potential. The desire to take on new challenges, assert their independence, and explore their identities is a natural extension of the same inner drive that propelled them through their early childhood milestones.

Taking Risks Is Important

Exploration and experimentation are keys to building resilience (aka mental toughness) and reducing anxiety. This statement may run counter to the attitude you've heard expressed by many of the parents and adults you've encountered, as sheltering and protecting young people from harm seems to have become a national pastime. A couple of generations ago, the big concerns parents had were about their kids using seatbelts, staying out past dark, or drinking alcohol. Now, in many families, rules have morphed into parents prohibiting their children from leaving the yard, engaging in physically rough play, and even working outside the home to make their own money.

Ours has become a world held hostage by the fear that children will be traumatized by average life events, simple events and activities that actually can make them more resilient and stronger. In effect, this kind of overprotection deprives young people of the essential lessons they need to function effectively in the real world.

Kids of all ages are naturally great at raising the stakes in their play. They know it gets boring doing the same old things. That's why they go from climbing on furniture and countertops to sliding down railings, climbing trees, and jumping their bikes off high places. They engage in a range of acceptably risky behaviors and, as a result, endure bumps, bruises, and scrapes—even an occasional broken bone. Through these experiences, they learn that minor hurts come with the territory of exploring themselves and the world. They start to understand what they can tolerate and what exceeds their limits. Essentially, they learn to get back up after being knocked down.

Kids are good at creating fun when things get boring or stale. They build ramps to jump their bikes off, climb trees to check for eggs in nests, make "slime" in the tub at their grandparents' house, take apart appliances to see how they work, dare their siblings to sit in a dark room that's supposed to be haunted (hoping for a scare), and try to get around rules like not sneaking food into their rooms late at night.

If you have done one or all of these things (I know I did many of them when I was young), you aren't alone. As you start to realize how big, fun, scary, inspiring, and exciting the world is, it makes you want to check it all out!

Today, the term *trauma* is often used to describe challenging experiences that leave a lasting and painful emotional impact. Listening to some people tell it, you'd think the younger generation is traumatized by just about everything. And of course, this is not true! However, the belief that they are and the design of overly restrictive childhood environments may reflect a more fundamental issue: Our society is so fear-based these days that it casts the world as a terrifying place where serious injury and child abductors lurk on every street corner.

The irony is that young people themselves don't often develop anxiety from simply exploring, taking risks, and pushing themselves to their natural limits. It is their parents who feel the most anxious. But you would think that teenagers do, given the news stories, opinion pieces, and testimonials provided on

Instagram and TikTok. Often, stories about danger involve dealing with horrific parents and abusive teachers, or encountering predatory strangers in ways that left them racked with fear and unable to function. Yet, this isn't really how most people become anxious or develop phobias.

Often anxiety doesn't arise from negative experiences alone; rather, it stems from a lack of exposure to everyday challenges and the resulting inability to handle them. Exposure to these difficult, but manageable events teaches children skills like tolerating discomfort, understanding that you won't be destroyed or killed by it, and learning mechanisms for coping with it. Because it takes time to learn from experience, exposure therapy, which is a form of *cognitive behavioral therapy* (CBT), involves exposing individuals who are struggling emotionally to feared situations and things gradually, resulting in reduced fear over a period of time.

The therapy works because it is gradual and split into steps of increasing difficulty, mirroring what kids do when they play. At each point, the person learns that feared negative events don't happen, but that, if they do, they will be able to tolerate and handle them. In the end, what emerges is a more confident and empowered individual who isn't afraid to take on new challenges.

Here's the best news: CBT techniques are effective for everyone, whether or not they have a history of trauma or clinical issues. The human central nervous system is built for exactly this kind of learning.

The idea of being "traumatized" or having a mental disorder because of something someone said or a typical childhood event, like being reprimanded by a teacher, is often an exaggeration. Casually using the word *traumatized* may reflect a mindset that views the world as threatening and sees oneself as unable to cope. This isn't to say teens don't experience real trauma—it's just that using this term incorrectly can dilute its meaning and confuse others trying to understand what you're going through.

It's similar to saying, "I'm so OCD" or "That's just my ADHD" when describing everyday experiences. Misusing psychological jargon makes it harder for you to express yourself clearly and accurately, which can lead to real feelings of confusion and disconnection from those who matter. Instead of saying, "I'm traumatized," try saying something more precise such as:

"I'm feeling disappointed."

"I'm really sad."

"My feelings are hurt."

"I'm upset and scared."

"I'm angry because this seems unfair to me."

"This is hard and I'm frustrated."

There are many words for emotional states that you can use, and it can be fun to study this vocabulary and practice using them in conversation. Naming your feelings helps you solve problems because it's the first step in learning how to manage them. Real resilience comes from facing challenges—and feelings—learning from them, and continuing to move forward despite setbacks. Resilience is built on the ability to manage your emotions.

All the testing, experimenting, and challenging of the status quo around you that you do is important. It is preparing you for your future as an adult. This transitional stage in your life isn't just about getting taller or smarter. It's also about becoming someone who makes things happen for yourself. Your brain and body are learning about themselves. Figuring out what they can do will help you tackle challenges and seize opportunities you can't even see yet.

To achieve our aims we usually need to stay calm under pressure. Your inner Warrior has the potential to become a master of self-restraint. Panicking while you try to balance yourself on a rickety bridge over a canyon does no one any good. Your Warrior self gets this basic fact, that a battle, whether it is the "battle" of getting permission to stay out late or drive the family car to the concert, can be decided against your favor by one or two moments of impulsiveness and a loss of cool.

Right now, each day, the Warrior in you is practicing, testing, and troubleshooting how to be more assertive, confident, and wise with your abilities. You may have learned to speak up at a younger age in certain situations like asking for a ride to a friend's house, telling a teacher you were having trouble with a math problem, or owning up to a mistake and apologizing to a friend. But now you are older and getting ready for the next level, which involves venturing out into the world under your own steam. No one is telling you where to go, what to like, and what choices to make about your future anymore. (Okay, maybe there are people doing this, but you are still the one who will make the final decision.) For example, you are the one signing on the dotted line or raising your hand to volunteer.

Given the fact of your growing independence, you need to learn how to take control of the direction of your day. And how to make decisions for yourself and live with them, even when the results turn out wrong. You are learning how to correct mistakes and learn as much as you can from them. You are doing all of this while shouldering more academic, family, social, and work responsibilities than you have ever taken on before in your life. This is pretty amazing.

Adolescence can feel like an awkward and uncertain time. You are changing physically, which means that maybe you get a little clumsy at times, struggle with clothes that no longer fit, and start having people treat you differently than they did just a few months ago. You are also changing psychologically. You are learning to control your feelings more, measure your words before using them, and anticipate how others will interpret what you do and say so that you can adjust your behavior accordingly. Now is a time when different strengths, like these, are coming into clearer focus for you.

A tendency to see the positives in even the most difficult situations, the ability to tolerate discomfort—even physical pain—in order to accomplish something important, and having the daring to push yourself to persevere will be abilities that help you act when you need to, and act without hesitation when you know deep inside what to do. These extraordinary skills will serve you more and more, in countless ways.

The Warrior

Each time you step outside your comfort zone, you draw on your inner Warrior. The Warrior in you can tolerate discomfort, confusion, and disappointment because it knows that difficult times are temporary. Plus, it knows that it is reasonable to sacrifice physical comfort and endure mental stress for a higher purpose. The Warrior is astutely aware of even the smallest infringement on your personal reality by negativity and oppression. Like a watchguard in a tower, the Warrior keeps an eagle eye on your personal freedom and will fight fiercely to maintain it. The Warrior is geared toward getting you up and out into the world, giving you the chance to discover what you are truly capable of.

Your Warrior side refuses to let others define you within their limited ideas of who you are or can become. It rebels against anyone who tells you that you aren't good enough or need to behave in a certain way. The Warrior will not allow you to be diminished by anyone or anything. This Champion is about action, about taking steps to clear the way for your strongest self to emerge. When clouds of negativity or darkness begin to overtake your thinking, the Warrior stands with its torch raised, banishing these forces so they can't influence your thinking.

Your Warrior side will urge you to take on challenges that stretch your courage and determination. These experiences help you grow in these areas knowing you will benefit in the long run. The Warrior within also holds a strong commitment to personal values and living intentionally, often demonstrating strength through peaceful and thoughtful action.

Imagine someone who decides to speak the truth in a group despite the possibility of exclusion or someone who needs to have a tough conversation with a friend about a troubling issue. Everyday moments like these can make us want to shrink and hide to avoid them. Avoiding conflict and trying to please people are two kinds of issues that a lot of adults struggle with—not only teens. The idea of putting our thoughts and feelings out in the open for the judgment of others and risking rejection would give almost anyone second thoughts. Believe it or not, these are just the sorts of moments that call for the Warrior in you. Like standing at the top of a dizzyingly high ladder prepared to climb down to safety from a burning building, the Warrior knows you have to do that which frightens you to be free from things that can harm you.

The Warrior spirit shows itself in everyday life, such as standing up to a bully or speaking out about community issues like homelessness. You may draw on your inner Warrior when you face your fears, like auditioning for a school play despite intense nerves or trying out for the basketball team even though you know you're not the best player.

Whether you're joining a debate club or a rock-climbing club, you may have nerves at the beginning. Standing up to do public speaking might bring up some feelings of shyness. Confronting a steep rock face for the first time may arouse your fear of heights. In either case, you are challenging yourself. The Warrior can help you tap in to the reason you wanted to do it in the first place. Maybe you want to be a good speaker because of how it will help you be an activist for causes you care about. Perhaps you want to climb rocks for the pure joy of athleticism and exhilaration of standing on the top of a mountain catching the views from on high. The moments of conquering your initial trepidation may appear minor, but as your successes accumulate, they will greatly advance your personal power and positively influence how you see yourself.

Each act of bravery and every decision to take on a challenge or overcome an obstacle will lay another brick in the foundation of your confidence and self-respect. Over time, such experiences can help you build an identity that is respected and appreciated, and positively influences those around you.

The Warrior tells you it is okay to listen to your desire, whether your passion is for painting, learning a new instrument, or creating videos for a YouTube channel. Your Warrior has your back and will fight to the end when it comes to expressing yourself and following the guidance of your heart.

The Warrior Mindset

The Warrior mindset incorporates two critical psychological practices, mindfulness and radical acceptance, each of which plays a key role in fostering resilience and emotional intelligence.

Mindfulness. This aspect of the Warrior mindset involves maintaining a moment-by-moment awareness of your thoughts, feelings, bodily sensations, and surrounding environment. Mindfulness is about being fully present without distraction or judgment. When you practice mindfulness, you cultivate the ability to observe your experiences objectively.

For example, during a challenging discussion in a class at school, mindfulness would help you not to react impulsively to a provocative comment from a student that disagrees with you. Instead, you could pause, breathe deeply, and observe your immediate emotional reactions and thoughts. This pause would allow you to respond thoughtfully and less reactively than you might have done otherwise, demonstrating a controlled and respectful engagement with both the topic and your peers.

Radical acceptance. Radical acceptance is a mental stance that goes hand in hand with mindfulness but has to do with how you relate to your experiences. The mindset of fully accepting your current situation—no matter what it is—without trying to change it does not necessarily mean you agree with or condone a negative circumstance or aspect of your life; rather, it means you acknowledge how things are at this moment.

For teens, radical acceptance might mean recognizing that although not being invited to a certain social event, such as a birthday party or group outing, is disappointing and hurtful, it doesn't define your worth or determine your social life forever. Instead of denying your feelings or overreacting to circumstances, you accept your emotions as valid responses to the situation. This stance can reduce your suffering and open space for constructive action, like reaching out to others or addressing a misunderstanding directly.

Together, mindfulness and radical acceptance empower you to face life with a clear, unclouded mind. They help manage emotions by not allowing initial gut reactions to control your actions, thus enhancing decision-making skills. This combination supports personal growth and emotional resilience and improves interpersonal relationships by promoting a more compassionate, patient, and understanding approach to interactions.

The Warrior mindset helps you:

- Lean In to Challenges. When faced with a big project or a tough exam, you don't shy away. Instead, you dive in and tackle it bit by bit. You face challenges head on, acknowledging their difficulty while committing to working through them piece by piece. This approach exemplifies the Warrior's mindset of persistent engagement and resilience.

- Embrace Discomfort. Growth often means stepping out of what's comfortable. Whether it's speaking up in class when you're usually shy or trying a new sport, embracing discomfort is key. It's okay to feel awkward or nervous because these experiences are crucial for growth. Here, the Warrior mindset embraces radical acceptance, recognizing, and accepting feelings without judgment.

- Accept Setbacks. Setbacks are a part of everyone's life. Perhaps a test doesn't go as planned or you've had an argument with a friend. True heroism requires heroic efforts. This means not being deterred by these hurdles— whether it involves apologizing and trying to understand your friend's perspective or consulting your teacher on how to improve your grades. By taking active steps forward, you embody the Warrior's resilience, overcoming fear, self-doubt, and avoidance.

- Grow Stronger Through Adversity. Being strong and resilient isn't just about recovering from a fall; it's about growing stronger and wiser from it. Like how a muscle strengthens with exercise, your resilience builds with every hurdle faced. Each setback is not just a challenge but a training opportunity for future challenges, helping you develop a durable, adaptable character.

By understanding and embracing your inner Warrior, you will find the strength and courage to tackle life's challenges, grow from experience, and become the best version of yourself that's possible.

The Spoiler

All of us have built in survival instincts designed to prevent us from heading into dangerous situations we cannot handle. These instincts help prevent overconfidence, serving as the part of us that is critical, doubting, and always watching out for problems. But imagine this part falling into a nuclear vat, transforming into a radioactive mutant version of itself. This mutated instinct, which we'll call the Spoiler, is a member of the Dark Legion that feeds off fear by creating a constant sense of impending doom in your mind.

The Spoiler excels at instilling you with self-doubt, fear of failure, and the pressure to conform and stay safe. The Spoiler sows seeds of doubt in your abilities and decisions and leads you to second-guess expressing your true self. Making you the false promise of keeping you safe, the Spoiler convinces you to conform to what you imagine others consider cool or normal. (You might be wrong about that!)

In exchange for this false promise of security, you compromise your true feelings and self-expression, imprisoning yourself in a cage of inhibition and repression that keeps you small and weakened—right where the Spoiler wants you. To free yourself from the Spoiler's grip, the Warrior knows you must face your fears and embrace your true self, even if it means doing something that frightens you a little or a lot.

The Spoiler's goal is to diminish your potential by making you feel afraid, timid, and reluctant to explore new interests. It aims to spoil your sense of self-worth by making you feel as if your opinions don't matter, that you have no right to speak up for your beliefs, and that expressing them will only lead to ridicule and rejection. The Spoiler wants you to believe that you are not strong enough to handle rejection or disagreement—or that the pain of these experiences would overwhelm and destroy you. Rejection and the power of other people's opinions are depicted as destructive forces that you must avoid and shape your life around.

As a result, the Spoiler turns you into someone who tells others what you think they want to hear or whatever you believe will please them, despite any personal cost to you. Disagreement becomes something too painful to bear. "You will risk becoming a nuisance, a bad person, or even crazy when you give voice to an opinion that differs from what is popular," the Spoiler tries to teach you.

The Spoiler sets unrealistic expectations about the grades you get on your schoolwork, your looks, and your level of popularity, making you feel like you're never good enough, not trying hard enough, or not caring enough about others. The perfect images and lifestyles we see on social media, TV, and other media in the current world only reinforce our impossible-to-achieve standards. Not getting perfect grades, not getting into a top college, or not being invited to hang out with popular peers is equated to being a failure if you believe what the Spoiler says. Things like:

"If you were smart, you would be like X, Y, or Z."

"If you want to be truly happy, you'll need to have X, Y, or Z."

Lies. Lies. Lies. Comparison and perfectionism are weapons used to bludgeon you into becoming a smaller version of yourself.

In your mind, the Spoiler often paints self-repression as a "noble" action, suggesting to you that concealing your true feelings and opinions is merely being considerate of others, or "not selfish," or that it demonstrates openness. However, this manipulation, which you do to yourself, diminishes your self-worth. In time, you may even come to dislike yourself for having conformed to living in a manner that doesn't match what you really thought and felt. This approach weakens you, making you more susceptible to external influences and exploitation, and prioritizes external approval over genuine self-expression.

If you have clarity about your aspirations, the Spoiler will attempt to dismiss them as trivial or misguided, labeling the pursuit of your dreams as foolish rather than brave. This tactic of dictating how you should spend your time by warping the definitions of what is "important" and what constitutes a "waste of time" is about control.

The Spoiler contaminates your thinking and feeling by filling your mind with negative thoughts and emotions. It clouds your judgment, making you believe that you are less capable and worthy than you truly are. This mental contamination leads to a cycle of negativity, where every small setback feels like a monumental failure, and every criticism feels like a personal attack. The Spoiler amplifies your fears and insecurities, making it difficult to see your strengths and potential. If you cannot find a way to silence the Spoiler's voice in your head, its constant bombardment of negative thoughts and emotions can leave you feeling overwhelmed, anxious, and paralyzed, unable to move forward or make decisions confidently.

Sadly, the Spoiler not only can undermine your confidence, but it can also spoil your experiences and relationships because of how it feeds on your self-doubt and preys on your insecurity. Let's say you're working on a group project at school and you have an idea that could solve a problem, but just before you speak up, you start worrying that your idea will seem foolish to your cohort. As a result, you stay quiet and the conversation moves on without your contribution. In that moment, when the Spoiler wins, your cohort loses out on the benefit of hearing your special perspective. They might decide you're not someone they can rely upon and base all their future interactions with you on that idea. You might lose friends.

Every time the Spoiler wins, you miss a chance to express yourself and make an impact. Recognizing when you're being tempted to stay silent and choosing to share your thoughts anyway helps you fight back against the Spoiler, making you stronger and more confident in expressing your opinions.

The Spoiler also spoils your future prospects by fostering the fear of failure. It magnifies the risks and downplays the rewards of taking chances, convincing you that staying within your comfort zone is safer. This may prevent you from trying new things, learning from mistakes, and growing as a person. It could keep you from asking for things you want, going out for a team, traveling, applying to a better college, putting in an application for a job, or inviting someone you really like out on a date. By keeping you trapped in a state of fear and self-doubt, the Spoiler will rob you of numerous opportunities for personal and professional growth.

By contrast, the Warrior honors your genuine thoughts and feelings. If this were a videogame, the Spoiler would be that mutant boss run amok that the Warrior must subdue. But it is not. Even so, the battle is real. Your inner Warrior must reject the narrow definitions imposed on you by your inner Spoiler. The Warrior knows your capabilities and potential and cannot be fooled.

Embracing your true self empowers you to unleash the Warrior within, which sets a powerful example for those around you. That is a noble objective. So, be sure to ask yourself about the life you would really love to seek. Do you want to live in a way that might impress others but leaves you feeling hollow, or to have a life filled with genuine passion? The second is going to be more fun and rewarding for you ultimately.

Choosing to follow your passions will be a direct challenge to the Spoiler's agenda of fear and conformity. It involves redefining what is important and being responsible for going after it. It means pursuing authenticity over security and personal fulfillment over societal approval. But the beauty in this path is that the people you befriend and surround yourself with will be likeminded and value the same things that you do.

To reinforce the stance of authenticity, you will need to explore unconventional models of success. For example, you might consider the businessperson who values work-life balance over relentless career progression or the artist whose style disrupts mainstream norms. Diversity can be interesting. Study community leaders who focus on making a meaningful local impact rather than chasing national fame. Such individuals are deeply connected to their communities and often enjoy the mutual respect of those they respect and care for. Instead of striving for popularity on a mass level with strangers who don't know them personally, their careers illustrate that fulfillment comes from alignment with personal values, like civic responsibility and community well-being.

By investigating and celebrating alternative paths as well as traditional paths, in time you will learn what best suits your aspirations. With each Warrior step you take, you break free from another of the constraints with which the Spoiler has bound you. You can become a role model for the next guy, too. Your acts of courage not only will validate your self-worth but they may also inspire others to live authentically, creating a ripple effect of empowerment and leadership all around you.

Being Assertive vs. Being Selfish

It's a common misconception that it's selfish for young people to assert themselves, carve out their own spaces, and expect respect from others. However, pursuing your genuine interests is not only critical to your happiness and ultimate success in life, but it is also fundamentally right to do. Ignoring or rejecting your own ideas only supports the Spoiler's false narrative that self-neglect is noble. Conversely, being assertive is what makes it possible for you to make your unique contributions to the world.

Claiming your space doesn't detract from others claiming theirs; rather, it enhances the collective well-being and fosters a more vibrant, supportive community. You are at your best when you're going the extra mile to make things happen, doing what you truly love to do.

In today's society, so-called cancel culture and a mob mentality often discourage individuals from expressing their true opinions and preferences. *Mob mentality* refers to the way individuals in a group can be influenced to adopt certain behaviors, follow trends, and enforce conformity by having everyone else agree to gang up on them simultaneously. This is a painful experience for the person being controlled in this manner, one that often leads to the suppression of individual opinions and actions. *Cancel culture* refers to the mob's decision to ruin a person's life and livelihood.

External forces like mobs and a culture of malice and punishment amplify the inner Spoiler's voice, creating a hostile environment where unique contributions are stifled.

The ability to explore ideas and beliefs openly, to disagree without being labeled or subjected to hostility and rejection, is increasingly compromised in our society. Yet, standing firm in your authenticity and pursuing your passions is a powerful counter to this kind of negativity. By staying true to yourself and by showing respect for the right of others to stay true to themselves—even when you disagree with them—you will challenge the toxic dynamics of cancel culture and the mob mentality, potentially inspiring others to do the same and ultimately contributing to a healthier and more diverse community.

The Power of Incremental Progress

To begin combating the Spoiler, start by reaching for what is often called the "low-hanging fruit" in your life. This means setting your sights on tasks or goals that are easiest to achieve and require the least effort. By addressing these first, you can quickly make progress and build momentum for more complex challenges.

In the movie *The Karate Kid*, a boy named Daniel moves from New York City to California. As he tries to settle in to the neighborhood, he encounters a terrifying group of bullies who repeatedly harass and try to intimidate him. One day, his neighbor, Mr. Miyagi, steps in to physically defend Daniel when he is being beaten up. Mr. Miyagi, an elderly man, easily defeats four young men proficient in martial arts. Amazed, Daniel asks Mr. Miyagi to teach him how to fight. Miyagi reluctantly agrees and asks Daniel to show up for training the next day.

When he does, Mr. Miyagi instructs Daniel to clean and wax his cars using a very specific motion with his hands ("wax on, wax off"). The next day, hoping the real training would begin, Daniel returns only to have Miyagi instruct him to paint his enormous fence, again using a particular set of brush strokes that flex his wrists up and down. This goes on for a few days until Daniel, frustrated, finally confronts Miyagi, exclaiming, "What the hell has this got to do with fighting?!"

In response, Miyagi asks Daniel to demonstrate the motions he's been practicing—the wax-on, wax-off motions and the up-down fence-painting movements—but this time without a rag or a brush. As Daniel performs the motions he learned, Miyagi throws punches and kicks at him, which Daniel instinctively blocks. In this moment, Daniel realizes that Miyagi had been training him to do karate all along through having him perform repetitive tasks and build his muscle memory. Miyagi knew that if he had explained the purpose behind the tasks, Daniel might not have believed him or engaged with the exercises with the necessary diligence.

By trusting Miyagi's unconventional methods, Daniel un-knowingly developed the foundational skills of self-defense, which just goes to show how effective and essential trust and patience are in learning new skills. Building off this lesson from *The Karate Kid,* can you appreciate that it's essential for you to start with small, seemingly simple actions to train your inner Warrior?

Reflect on moments when you have remained silent during a group discussion, and those when you have chosen to voice your opinion. Consider what contributed to either of those choices. Was there a time when you reached out to someone you might not usually engage with, such as a new classmate or a coworker at your afterschool job?

To build upon this small bit of progress you have already made, try to find new places where you could also share something personal about yourself, especially in settings where you'd typically be reserved, like at a community meeting or in an online forum. These acts may seem minor, but they are powerful gestures that can defend against even powerful bullies like the Spoiler. Each small step is a building block in developing your confidence and assertiveness, much like how Daniel's simple tasks built his martial arts skills.

Small changes, accumulating over time, can lead to significant transformations.

You can also draw inspiration from real-life leaders around the world who embody this principle. Take Martin Luther King, Jr., for example. He didn't simply wake up one day, decide to enter the ministry, and then immediately start marching for civil rights. His commitment to social change was the result of many years of personal growth, education, and gradual involvement in the civil rights movement. This development included his theological studies, his early sermons, and his deepening understanding of nonviolent protest. It's like the adage from Hollywood, "Every overnight success is ten years in the making." Often, we see only a small percentage of what has really gone into someone else's success. We typically don't see the reality and behind-the-scenes ordinariness of their daily lives.

The Myth of Effortless Success

The idea that we are inherently born to excel at something—that recognizing our innate talents and intelligence leads to automatic success—is a compelling narrative often reinforced in various ways. We marvel at prodigies who show extraordinary abilities, like a five-year-old mastering complex calculus or a young musician playing Beethoven like a seasoned professional. These stories captivate us, perpetuating the myth of effortless, predestined achievement.

That's why in this book, your inherent talents are celebrated, but it is also emphasized that automatic or immediate success is not assumed. Practicing, learning, adjusting, and adapting over time are requirements of mastering the skills and techniques of any pursuit. It is the rare occasion you reach your goal without these elements. Even if you are a child prodigy, a rigorous routine of practice and education will be key to your development.

The popular author Malcolm Gladwell discusses the 10,000-hour rule in his book *Outliers*. This principle (which he invented, by the way) states that mastering almost anything requires 10,000 hours of practice. While this might seem like a substantial amount of time, consider this: If you live to be ninety years old, 10,000 hours will be just over one percent of your entire life span. In the grand scheme of your life, that is a relatively small commitment.

Malala Yousafzai first became a global leader by taking on a monumental cause as a teen. She was shaped significantly by her early experiences in Swat Valley, Pakistan, where her father was a teacher and an educational activist. Her home environment fostered her love for education. From a young age, Malala was exposed to the challenges surrounding education rights, especially for girls, under the oppressive rule of the Taliban. Her father's influence and support played a crucial role in her becoming an advocate for education. At just eleven years old, Malala began blogging for the BBC about living under the Taliban's efforts to deny her an education. After surviving an assassination attempt, at age seventeen she was awarded the Nobel Peace Prize.

Malala stood strong against others who tried to undermine the fight for girls' education in regions where it's restricted or denied. She could have chosen to go with the flow, listen to the Spoiler, and not assert herself. She didn't, though. The fact that she and others like her were being denied an education and told they were not deserving only seemed to strengthen Malala's resolve to fight. Malala had a strong sense of what is right and refused to back down, day after day.

Others, like Martin Luther King, Jr., and Mahatma Gandhi—one of King's own role models—exemplify the same Warrior spirit through their peaceful resistance to oppression and advocacy for human rights. Despite facing severe consequences, each remained committed to nonviolence and civil disobedience. No moment or opportunity was wasted. They truly committed themselves to what they felt was important and right.

These humanitarian leaders deeply believed in peace and the rights of all people. They embodied these beliefs, even when it was tough and they had chances to give up their principles. Their strong commitment shows the kind of strength it takes to stick to nonviolent beliefs despite opposition and difficulties, inspiring future generations.

Warrior Training

Like these leaders, everyone must start somewhere. They began with small, important steps that anyone, including you, can take. By starting with just one step, you can begin a journey that leads to big changes.

You may not aspire to be the next great global leader, but you do have ambitions. Reflecting on the accomplishments of important leaders can show you what is possible, even if your goals differ from theirs.

This is why we start with what is right in front of you today. Things you might easily overlook and take for granted but can start on right away. We also don't want to throw you right into the deep end. Having unrealistic expectations is one of the best ways to wind up feeling discouraged and down on yourself. Your Warrior needs to train before it can go on to fight in the big leagues. It needs to learn how to fend for itself, anticipate obstacles, and develop the ability to improvise, like you might in a debate, negotiation, or an attempt to deescalate an argument between friends.

Focusing on personal and social boundaries is crucial because this is one of the biggest areas of growth happening during adolescence. By setting a solid foundation with the Warrior's help, you will build habits and relationships that uplift you. Be aware, using the Warrior's mindset, that with these micro-steps, you are conditioning your Warrior for the bigger battles.

Being a warrior in your own life doesn't always mean performing grand, cinematic acts. Often, it's the quiet, unseen actions that have the most impact. Whether it's giving up your seat for someone, letting someone cut in line, or including someone who's alone, these small acts help define you as a person. Stepping out of your comfort zone might feel risky, complete with nervousness and awkward moments, but you're merely stretching yourself—uncomfortable, yes, but rarely dangerous.

The training plan that follows will get your Warrior into action, on the playing field, and growing stronger day by day. The focus of these steps will be on areas of great importance to people in your age cohort, such as school, friendships, dating, family, and independence. Use this section to help you think about all the ways you can begin to grow more assertively and confidently into being your best, authentic self.

Exercise 1: Going After What You Want

The Warrior clears the path for you to pursue your true interests, even if they diverge from those of the crowd. It might be daunting to break away because of potential judgment or gossip and whispers, but being true to yourself—whether that means starting a school recycling program, skateboarding, or coding—sometimes requires bravery. Your inner Warrior supports you in being true to your passions, from knitting hats to starting fundraisers for causes you care about.

Instructions: Choose one passion or interest that you have been hesitant to pursue due to a fear of judgment. Take one small step toward pursuing it this week. This step can be as simple as researching the activity online, talking to someone who shares your interest, or starting a project.

Exercise 2: Establishing Boundaries

The world has a space just for you, but you must carve it out. Establishing psychological and emotional boundaries allows you to define and maintain your personal space, protecting you from being overwhelmed by external demands that conflict with your values.

Instructions: Reflect on a typical situation where you might feel overwhelmed by the demands of others. Practice how you can say no or express your needs in a respectful manner.

For instance, if a friend often will ask you to hang out when you need to study, practice explaining your situation and suggesting an alternative time. This will prepare you to handle the next situation when you feel like you might comply.

Exercise 3: Making Choices That Benefit You

The purpose of this exercise is to help make simple daily choices aligned with your best interests. Perhaps a friend invites you to a party, but you have planned a quiet evening to rest and recharge. Although it's tempting to say yes to avoid disappointment, what your body really needs is for you to say no. Understanding your true need (in this case, for rest) enables you to make a choice that will benefit you the most.

Instructions: Identify one decision you need to make this week where your preference might conflict with someone else's or a tempting possibility might conflict with your best interests. Practice making the choice that best aligns with your needs and explaining it clearly to others.

Exercise 4: Thoughtful Action and Inner Guidance

Importantly, your inner Warrior isn't about being impulsive or reckless. Its voice guides you to act thoughtfully. It connects with what's deep in your heart, amplifying it so you can't ignore your true desires and helps you plan and execute your "missions" successfully.

Instructions: Set a goal that requires thoughtful planning. Break it down into a series of small actions steps and create a timeline for their accomplishment.

For instance, if you want to organize a community event, outline the tasks involved, such as finding a location to hold the event, writing an email invitation, making flyers to post, and so forth, then assign deadlines for completing each one.

Start by taking the first step this week.

Exercise 5: Staying True to Yourself

Remember, you don't have to be a bystander in this world. Facing challenges or pressures that try to sway you, staying true to yourself is crucial. The cost of neglecting your beliefs and denying your true thoughts, feelings, preferences, background, and goals, among other things, is often much higher than the cost of honoring them, despite any opposition you may encounter.

Instructions: Identify a belief or value that you hold strongly. Reflect on how you can deliberately honor this belief in your daily life.

Take one action this week that reinforces your commitment to this value, such as standing up for a cause you believe in or practicing honesty in a difficult situation.

By starting with these two actions, you can begin to strengthen your inner Warrior, building the resilience and confidence needed to navigate life's challenges.

Final Thoughts on the Warrior

The process of embracing the Warrior within you is about recognizing and harnessing your growing power and potential. As you navigate the challenges of adolescence, your brain and body are not just preparing you to tackle new opportunities and obstacles, they are also igniting your latent natural powers. That is why this chapter has emphasized the significance of authenticity, assertiveness, and thoughtful action.

Remember, the journey of becoming your best self is a journey of taking small, but impactful steps. By focusing on what is right in front of you today, you will lay the foundation for greater achievements tomorrow. By doing the provided exercises, you can activate the neural circuits that correspond to the Warrior's personality traits, enhancing your brain's natural powers of resilience, confidence, and strategic thinking.

Furthermore, the Warrior within you will help you define your character in this stage of your life through quiet, everyday actions as much as grand acts of bravery. You only ever need to step slightly outside your comfort zone to build your confidence and sense of self.

CHAPTER THREE

....

THE WIZARD

In the early days, the Wizard engineered solutions to the problems of humankind and helped people see what could be, instead of what was. Human foresight and creativity birthed new inventions and ways of life, transforming society and pushing the boundaries of human potential. The Wizard grasped the boundless potential within every individual, understanding that each person possesses the innate power to innovate and imagine beyond their wildest dreams.

As the Mastermind of your life, you want to turn your dreams into reality. To do this, you must first envision what your ideal life looks like. Who will be in it and what will you be doing every day? This envisioning process taps into the part of you that I call the Wizard.

A little girl named Anya loved birds. She especially enjoyed watching the crimson cardinals that visited the bird bath in her family's backyard and geese flying in formation during their annual fall migration to a warmer climate. When she would see a flock passing overhead, Anya would point up at them and ask her mom all sorts of questions about where they were going and what it felt like to fly. This created the opportunity for her mother to talk with her and make comparisons to airplanes and other forms of travel used by humans. She would explain to her daughter that observing how the natural world functions can teach us valuable lessons and suggest methods for solving problems and accomplishing tasks.

As she grew older, Anya's sense of wonder stayed with her. She carried her enthusiasm for learning into her school years, always feeling eager to discover more about the world. Even when things got a little tough, like when she struggled with frustration in her eighth-grade math class, she maintained a spark of curiosity and love for discovery. Anya was enamored with animals and collected books about dogs, cats, and underwater sea creatures, pouring over them at night, thinking about the places they lived and the fascinating ways they had found to survive in the wild. At one point, a science project using potatoes to generate electricity led to a newfound fascination with renewable energy. She eagerly shared her discovery with her classmates and teacher, turning the entire classroom into a mini science lab filled with potato batteries.

This particular project ignited a passion in Anya for environmental science, leading her to join the high school's science club. There, she participated in various experiments and projects, always looking for new ways to explore and understand the world around her. Her enthusiasm was contagious, inspiring her friends to join her in different scientific adventures. These early adventures also taught her patience and perseverance, as she learned that sometimes you must wait and watch to see something truly amazing, like when robin chicks in a nest just outside her window finally hatched from their eggs.

Through the years, Anya's appetite for exploration led her to take on new hobbies and interests. She started a nature journal, recording her observations of the world around her. This turned into a kind of scavenger hunt where she kept track of the birds in her neighborhood, and the times of year when she saw them. Anya started to see how seasons influenced the natural world, leading to migration patterns and a variety of other natural phenomena. She noticed how birds would fly south for the winter, how certain plants would bloom only in spring, and how animals would adapt their behaviors to survive the changing conditions.

Anya's appreciation for the intricate balance of nature deepened and sparked a lifelong interest in environmental science. Her sense of interconnectedness with all living things deepened as she participated in community service projects, working with her friends to improve the local environment and to support wildlife conservation efforts. She shared her love with her peers by encouraging them to join her in these activities, fostering a sense of community and shared purpose.

Before she graduated high school, Anya had applied all these lessons from observing nature in various ways. When she faced challenges in school, she would remember the patience she learned from watching the grass wave in the wind and the perseverance she gained from observing the birds. She approached her studies with the same curiosity she had as a much younger child, eager to learn something new.

The lens through which each of us views reality can be reconfigured in innumerable ways, like a kaleidoscope. You, like Anya, have a Wizard side. It is a force of nature, a beacon of creative energy, innovative thinking, and boundless imagination, and one of humankind's most powerful champions. Anya's Wizard side introduced her to the wonders of scientific discovery and environmental innovation. Just as the Wizard that resided inside each of our ancestors at some point introduced humanity to fire, the wheel, and the written word, Anya's Wizard propelled her from mere appreciation of nature to active exploration and protection of it by inspiring her to delve into environmental science and participate in local conservation efforts with enthusiasm and creativity.

Developing Your Wizarding Traits

As a young child, your Wizard was free from the constraints of rules, goals, or others' expectations. Experimentation, testing ideas, and pushing boundaries were your daily pursuits. If you were lucky, you were allowed to explore the world, at times unsupervised, allowed to trip and fall, to deal with frustration, and to feel how long it takes and the work needed to reach a goal, whether that was building a sandcastle, fixing a chain that had come loose on your bike, or learning to do a cartwheel. This type of learning is essential when it comes to everything, including relationships and socializing.

Experts across various fields agree that free play is essential for healthy development at all ages. *Free play* is any activity that is enjoyed for its own sake, without any purpose. Developmental psychologists like Jean Piaget and Lev Vygotsky emphasize that play helps us understand and navigate the world. Piaget believed that through play, we absorb new information and experiences, which helps our brain grow and learn. The brain never stops evolving, due to a phenomenon known as *plasticity*. Vygotsky highlighted that play lets you practice skills just beyond your current abilities, helping you improve and learn in a social context.

There are a couple of researchers I admire who have done work on play that might interest you. Psychiatrist Stuart Brown, M.D., founder of the National Institute for Play, says that play is crucial for managing emotions, relieving stress, and developing empathy. He sees play as a basic human need that shapes our brains, brings joy, and helps us connect with others. You can watch him talk about play in his TED Talk at TED.com.

Similarly, the research of neuroscientist and psychobiologist Jaak Panksepp, Ph.D., shows that play triggers the brain's reward system, releasing dopamine into the bloodstream, which makes us feel good and reinforces our learning. You can watch him talk about play in his TEDx Talk posted on YouTube.com.

Here's what we know so far. Play isn't just about having fun. It's vital for your social, emotional, cognitive, and physical growth. Through play, you learn to handle your emotions, cope with stress, and build resilience. It also helps you develop social skills like cooperation, negotiation, and resolving conflicts. The American

Academy of Pediatrics emphasizes that unstructured playtime is crucial for sparking creativity and imagination. Free play allows you to explore and discover, giving you a sense of connection and belonging.

In essence, free play is more than just a break from structured activities; it's a powerful tool for growth and development. Whether you're playing sports, creating art, or just hanging out with friends, play provides an opportunity for self-exploration and discovery, free from the pressures of performance and judgment.

Animal models of play, such as the model of tiger cubs play fighting by biting each other and their parents, demonstrate how play prepares them for real-world challenges. While it's clear that these behaviors are related to hunting skills and self-defense, they also serve a less obvious but equally important purpose. Through play, tiger cubs learn how to socialize with each other, discovering what is too much, where the boundary between play and aggression lies, and how to repair relationships when they have gone too far or messed up. This play also gives them a sense of connection and belonging within their family group.

And really, it's not so different for us humans. I'm pretty sure I wasn't the only one who sometimes resembled a gorilla, a runaway elephant, or a wild dog when playing with friends. Just take a look at any park, playground, or schoolyard, and tell me it doesn't look like a jungle out there. Kids swinging like monkeys, stampeding like loose elephants, and forming packs like wild wolves. Sound like you and your siblings? Or maybe you and your friends?

When humans engage in play, in addition to being fun it also serves as a creative endeavor and an opportunity for self-exploration and discovery. However, when we start to perform and cultivate a particular brand or image to influence how others perceive us, it stops our play from being play and turns our play into a job. This shift transforms what should be a purely natural and beneficial activity into a potential source of anxiety and fear.

Dean Kamen:
A Modern-day Wizard

Dean Kamen epitomizes the modern-day Wizard, embodying the spirit of innovation, learning, and exploration. Born on April 5, 1951, in Rockville Centre, New York, from a young age Kamen was fascinated by technology and engineering. His father, an illustrator for EC Comics and *MAD Magazine,* encouraged his curiosity and creativity. Kamen attended Worcester Polytechnic Institute in Massachusetts, but left before graduating to focus on his inventions. His early career took off with the development of the AutoSyringe, a portable infusion pump that revolutionized drug delivery in healthcare. This invention laid the foundation for his first company, AutoSyringe, Inc., which he later sold to Baxter Healthcare.

Kamen's innovative spirit didn't stop there. He went on to invent the iBOT Mobility System, a revolutionary wheelchair capable of climbing stairs, and the Segway PT, a self-balancing personal transporter unveiled in 2001. His other notable inventions include the Slingshot, a water purification system designed for developing countries, and the DEKA Arm, an advanced prosthetic arm.

Recognizing that the next generation will need to address difficult challenges, Kamen has dedicated himself to promoting STEM education. (STEM is short for science, technology, engineering, and mathematics.) He founded the organization For Inspiration and Recognition of Science and Technology (FIRST) in 1989 to inspire young people to become science and technology leaders. FIRST offers programs like the FIRST Robotics Competition, FIRST LEGO League, and FIRST Tech Challenge, engaging students in hands-on, mentor-based programs that build STEM skills and inspire innovation.

Kamen clearly understands the importance of free play in healthy development. His initiatives encourage young people to engage in creative problem-solving and technological exploration in a playful manner. His philosophy is clear: The ability to experiment, push boundaries, and explore ideas freely is crucial for personal and societal advancement. He under-stands that true innovation comes from nurturing our innate curiosity and passion, much like the free play that develop-mental psychologists advocate.

Dean Kamen's journey from a young inventor to a globally recognized advocate for STEM education highlights his enduring commitment to improving lives through technology and inspiring future generations. His work demonstrates how the principles of play—exploration, creativity, and discovery—

are vital for fostering innovation and addressing the world's challenges. Through his inventions and educational initiatives, Kamen continues to nurture the next generation to embrace their Wizarding aspects by equipping them with the tools and mindset to make meaningful contributions to society.

The Wizarding World Today

As we have discussed, in today's digital age, a significant portion of our lives is spent online. This reality has created a unique environment where the desire to engage in activities for likes, shares, and views, has become a common experience. Nowhere else in the social world can you get this kind of rapid feedback. These metrics are seen as marks of acceptance, admiration, and respect, and they are instantly visible in the online world, unlike in real life where social validation takes more time and effort to achieve.

In our competitive, success-driven culture, there is immense pressure to be the best, gain approval, and avoid offending anyone. This environment can create significant distractions, making it difficult to engage in activities purely for enjoyment or personal interest. Instead, there is a constant need to perform and excel, which can shift the focus from internal motivation to seeking validation outside of yourself from others. This pressure stifles creativity and turn what should be playful and fulfilling experiences into stressful and anxiety-inducing tasks. The Wizard's approach, however, encourages focusing on growth and learning rather than just winning or pleasing others.

Developing traits of the Wizard is more challenging today than it used to be, primarily because of the context we find ourselves in. We are living in two different worlds, one online and the other physical. This means that you can be sucked into a black hole of online distractions whenever you turn on an electronic device. You may also be bombarded by information and images meant for adults, exposed to this material too soon and in overwhelming quantity. Because of the pace of the constant flow of stimulation, it can be challenging to give your own ideas space to develop.

In general, consumers of media today want to receive everything immediately, so the minds of people in our society are forgetting how to wait. Silence is rare. Many people are so unaccustomed to hearing the sound of their own thoughts that silence is uncomfortable to them. If your patience is short, it may be because you don't have a clear idea of all the work and people behind the finished products you view.

When you see six-pack abs on a smiling young person in a post on Instagram or in a TikTok video, you aren't seeing what they did to achieve this physique. You don't see that they only eat chicken and broccoli. Nor can you know if they are taking metabolic drugs that are damaging their systems. All for likes, shares, and views.

It's hard not to feel envious of attractive people in magazine advertisements who seem "perfect" according to the standards of our media-obsessed society. And that's kind of the point. You're supposed to want to run out and get the new kind of shampoo or supplement they want to sell you. Looking at such images, you are left to think you do have the discipline or genetics to do what the model did, when in fact, most people do not.

You may imagine that this type of success at building abdominal muscles is common and question what is wrong with you if you are unable to achieve it in a week or two of accelerating your workouts. This kind of distorted thinking is a direct result of exposure to the unrealistic and limited images your mind becomes saturated with when you spend time online, surfing social networks.

You may also find that you amass tons of knowledge online, but have trouble putting it together to create a clear and realistic picture of things in your head. You may feel confused and distressed by the seeming contradictions and inconsistencies of what you have learned because you don't have the experience to understand the context of the information.

Culture is like this. In other countries, you may know that people bow to each other as a form of respect. Yet, it is hard to tell which people to bow to, when you should bow, or how deeply to bow. You don't know this because the act of bowing occurs within a framework of rules, of which bowing is only a part. This is what happens when we take on lots of information without understanding it in context.

By the way, this is why we have conspiracy theories and flaky ideas about vaccinations containing microdevices that the government uses to monitor our every action. When taken in pieces, the ideas seem plausible, but when you flesh out how this would happen in the real world, the whole notion of conspiracies falls apart. If you have only been taught information without an application, your mind can run off in all kinds of wild directions.

The rules and laws you need to learn can only be learned through experience and exposure to them in real time. Think about learning to ride a bike or how to perform a dance move. You can read about these things—even get so knowledgeable that you can explain them inside and out to others. Does it mean you can hop on a bike or hit the dance floor performing at the level of someone who has been doing it for months or even years? Nope.

This is what is happening to you every day online. Your thinking is being "programmed" by giving you only part of the information you need and too much of all kinds of information you don't need.

When you inevitably don't know what to do, where to start, or how to temper your expectations, it is easy to start to feel like a failure. You may wonder how you are going to make it on your own, and whether or not you will have the smarts or strength to do well in life. You might answer these internal questions with incomplete and incorrect information as well—information that is based upon your limited experiences of feeling overwhelmed, frustrated, and confused. These are feelings that most people your age feel as they begin to be more aware of the wider world around them. But experiences of overwhelm and confusion are not accurate reflections of reality or your true capabilities when you are given a chance to process information.

Let's say you are interested in dating and want to learn how to talk to the opposite sex. You watch YouTube videos to figure out what people have done before that was successful, and what you could say to someone you like that "works" and will make them interested in you. But how do you know if the advice you see is good advice?

First, who is to say the videos you're watching aren't staged, or just someone's unique personal experience, or that the advice is suited only for a small set of situations or a few people? You can go by likes and comments. For sure, that can tell you something. But does it tell you whether the information being provided is what you need, or whether it fits your personality and circumstances? Would it work for someone who has the kind of interests you have that you are looking to share with someone you are dating? Would the advice work at your stage of life, given that talking to someone age thirteen is different than talking to someone age eighteen? These questions are a bit trickier to answer.

Following someone else's dating advice is like having a juggler tell you how to juggle, then getting your own set of balls or pins and trying to juggle them on your own. Pretty soon, balls are bouncing off your head, getting lost under the couch, and knocking over lamps. Before you get good at it, you are so frustrated that you give up and decide you are untalented and hopeless. But is this assessment fair to you? Isn't it true that you are just new to the art of juggling and could use more practice?

Understanding that context in which to apply advice and information will be the key to your success. The environment, experiences, and circumstances you find yourself in will shape your ability to innovate, take risks, and grow, which is crucial in developing your Wizard traits. Recognizing the importance of context will help you set realistic expectations for yourself and appreciate the journey behind every success story.

And remember, success in life is ultimately not about being good at everything but about putting yourself in situations that will maximize your chance of success at the things you choose to do. By placing yourself in environments that support your goals and leveraging the strengths of those around you as well as your own, you will enhance your potential for achievement and growth.

Fool's Gold

In today's world, we often design our lives around achieving love and acceptance through accomplishments, possessions, and money. But this is like valuing fool's gold. *Fool's gold* is an old miner's term for pyrite, a shiny, metallic-looking rock that resembles real gold. The term metaphorically describes something that appears precious or promising but is actually worthless.

Instead of chasing the "fool's gold" of life, focusing on forming genuine connections with people and taking steps to understand the context of things that you are learning about will lead you to have meaningful and fulfilling experiences.

You will inevitably grow and evolve as a person throughout your life becoming more knowledgeable about certain things. There is a distinction between taking pride in the discipline and work that come with honing a craft you feel passionate about (whatever that is for you) and simply pursuing achievement, status, and financial security without taking any pride in the work.

As you will discover when you are holding down a job day after day, year after year, seeking external validation for its rewards is like digging for fool's gold. True fulfillment in a career comes from pursuing what you love for its own sake, finding joy in the process of doing it. For instance, if you love writing, aim to write because it brings you joy and helps you express yourself, not merely to get published or to become famous and popular. True fulfillment in a hobby is similar because you are not anticipating earning the money you need to pay your bills.

If you love basketball, play because you enjoy the game, not just to win trophies. Play to impress scouts if you're trying to earn a college scholarship, but don't forget that the reason you might qualify for one is that you're good at the sport because you love it and have the discipline to work on your skills. A player develops muscle memory from shooting at tens of thousands of hoops.

From an early age, the things you enjoy doing—skills like drawing, making music, or building—can be turned into competitive ventures. When you first draw a picture and seek your parents' approval, you're not looking for praise as much as love and validation. If you have siblings, you might try to make your creation stand apart from theirs to impress your parents and get more positive attention. This pattern continues as you grow older. Good grades become a way to gain the affection and admiration of adults. Winning in sports may provide you with feelings of power and respect as well as status. Such early experiences shape your understanding of achievement and its connection to being loved.

At the heart of achievement, money, fame, and materialism often lies the need to be seen, respected, and admired. While it would be oversimplifying to say these pursuits are *always* about seeking validation, they are often turned into opportunities to get it. As you grow into adulthood, the same desire for recognition and acceptance that you feel today could continue to drive many of your choices. Whether it's excelling in your career, acquiring wealth, or seeking fame, these pursuits could be rooted in a desire to feel valued and appreciated. It is worth examining your motivations and asking yourself, *What's in this for me?*

Your mind, like an inventor's workshop, is a sanctuary for creative thinking and emotional mastery. It is a space to test out your ideas, no matter how far-fetched or seemingly irrelevant they may be. Imagine the Wizard as someone like the character Q in a James Bond movie. Q is a genius inventor who creates all the gadgets and devices Bond uses on his spy missions. Q meticulously prepares for every mission, thinking through all possible scenarios and crafting ingenious solutions. Just like Q's lab, your mind is a place where you can safely experiment and have things go wrong—without incurring any real-world consequences.

Thinking through your options before you act upon any one idea can save you time and trouble and create fewer messes to clean up, and the mistakes you do make can be made without audience participation and commentary. Mental preparation allows you to be adaptable and ready for life.

While the character James Bond may exude confidence and suaveness, it is also due to Q's resourcefulness that he is successful in his missions. Similarly, the Wizard within you uses innovation and creativity, not only in the outside world, but also within your mental landscape, to meet whatever needs arise. As the Mastermind, you will instruct the Wizard as to your objectives, and the Wizard will respond with its innovations.

Imagine possessing advanced simulation technology that creates realistic, three-dimensional environments where you can interact with lifelike holographic projections. In the iconic science fiction TV series *Star Trek,* starships are equipped with holodecks—versatile simulation chambers capable of recreating a vast array of environments—where people can pretend to do all kinds of crazy things. Your mind has the equivalent of its own holodeck, your imagination, which is a mental simulation space where the Wizard serves as the master engineer.

Experiences Tailored to Your Imagination

The Wizard can tailor your mindset to suit your needs at any given moment. Attuned to your thoughts, feelings, and experiences, the Wizard expertly molds your mental environment to support you and your goals. Here's how the Wizard establishes specific spaces to assist you.

For emotional management, it creates:

- A Healing Retreat. When stress becomes overwhelming, the Wizard activates this sanctuary for recuperation, helping to cleanse negative thoughts and infuse positive affirmations.

- A Creative Oasis. Whenever you need to regain emotional balance, the Wizard conjures this space for activities like dancing, drawing, or singing, helping reset your mood.

For preparation and planning, it sets up:

- A Strategy Room. Facing an upcoming challenge? The Wizard prepares this sphere where you can visualize each step you'll take to move toward success, reducing anxiety.
- A Rehearsal Stage. Before tough conversations or social challenges, the Wizard sets up this stage for you to practice different scenarios, boosting your confidence.

And for self-confidence, it establishes:

- A Hall of Triumphs. In moments of self-doubt, the Wizard guides you to this hall, showcasing your "success file" —a collection of memories of your achievements that remind you of your capabilities.
- A Creative Studio. When contemplating major life decisions, the Wizard opens this studio to help you visualize your goals aligned with your values. This process strengthens your self-confidence by clearly mapping out your path to success and ensuring your decisions are deeply rooted in your personal values, giving you the assurance to move forward with conviction.

The Wizard is forward-thinking. Its top skill lies in shaping your mental space at your request, in creating adaptable environments that help you tackle daily challenges and seize opportunities. Whether you're dealing with peer pressure or the prospect of participating in volunteer work or weighing important personal decisions, the Wizard can help you think ahead about possible outcomes. This preparation empowers you to make decisions that truly align with who you are.

These special mental environments equip you to handle life's complexities with confidence and clear direction, turning every challenge into a chance for personal growth and discovery. Imagine these spaces like different rooms in a house, each designed for a specific task—there's a quiet study for reflection, a vibrant workshop for planning, and a cozy lounge for regaining peace of mind. Each "room" the Wizard creates helps you live your life more fully and intentionally.

The Distractor

Within your internal reality, the Dark Legion of psychological forces that may try to sabotage you includes a "specialist" dedicated to opposing the constructive influence of the Wizard. (Each of the Five Champions has an enemy like this.) While the Wizard creates environments that enhance your focus, productivity, and personal growth, the Distractor works tirelessly to undermine these efforts by shifting your attention to trivial or distressing matters.

The Distractor's main tactic is to divert you from your true interests by causing you to obsess over uncontrollable issues, particularly those which provoke negative emotions. It whispers thoughts of inadequacy in your ear, convincing you that you lack something essential and must seek fulfillment from external sources, creating in you a perpetual state of feeling incomplete or deficient.

The Distractor's distortions and false beliefs include the following things.

- Dependency. The Distractor convinces you that you can't handle life's challenges on your own, promoting the idea that happiness and contentment come from external aids such as material possessions, validation, or solutions from outside sources. It undermines your self-sufficiency, suggesting that life's obstacles are too big for you to overcome without these external crutches. This belief traps you in a cycle of constantly seeking approval and new possessions, leaving you perpetually unfulfilled and dependent, instead of building inner resilience and self-reliance.

- Conformity in Personal Attitudes. The Distractor tells you to follow the crowd because they supposedly know best. It makes you believe that fitting in and being like everyone else is the key to acceptance and success. This discourages you from embracing your unique qualities and pursuing your individual interests, leading to a loss of identity and personal satisfaction.

- Conformity in Creativity. The Distractor mocks original ideas, promoting fear of failure if you deviate from the norm. It discourages innovation and creative thinking by making you believe that unconventional ideas are risky and likely to fail. This stifles your creativity and prevents you from exploring new possibilities and solutions.

- Scarcity. The Distractor focuses on what you don't have, suggesting that you always need more. It creates a mindset of lack and insufficiency, making you feel that no matter what you achieve or acquire, it will never be enough. This belief drives you to constantly chase after more, instead of focusing on creating what your heart truly needs.

Everyday Differences Between the Wizard and the Distractor

Here are a few contexts in which you can draw distinctions between the Wizard's influence and the Distractor's influence on your thinking and attention.

Social media. The Wizard focuses on completing homework or a creative project, while the Distractor tempts you with endless scrolling through TikTok or Instagram, pulling your attention away from your goals. For example, you might intend to spend only a few minutes checking your social media, but find yourself still scrolling an hour later, having accomplished nothing meaningful.

Video games. While the Wizard encourages you to finish studying for a test, the Distractor lures you into playing "just one more level" of a video game, leading to procrastination and stress. You might end up spending hours gaming, neglecting your studies and ensuring that you feel unprepared for your test, which increases your anxiety and sense of inadequacy.

Group chats. The Wizard promotes engaging in meaningful conversations and activities, but the Distractor bombards you with constant notifications and trivial group chat discussions, making it hard to concentrate on important tasks. For instance, you might be trying to write an essay but keep getting distracted by messages about weekend plans, making it difficult to focus and complete your work.

Negative news. The Wizard seeks to keep you focused on positive and productive activities, while the Distractor fixates your mind on distressing news stories, increasing anxiety and diverting your focus. You might start your day intending to work on a project, but get sidetracked by reading about political turmoil or natural disasters, leaving you feeling hopeless and demotivated.

Peer drama. The Wizard helps you stay focused on your personal growth and responsibilities, whereas the Distractor pulls you into friends' conflicts or gossip, draining your emotional energy and time. Instead of preparing for a presentation, you might spend hours trying to mediate a friend's argument, leaving you stressed and unprepared.

These examples illustrate how the Distractor's false beliefs can manifest in everyday situations, diverting your attention and undermining your goals. Recognizing these patterns can help you stay focused and harness the power of the Wizard to achieve your aspirations.

The Distractor tries to keep you small, disempower you, and make you feel helpless. It wants you to think that solutions to how you feel lie in conspicuous consumption, financial success, and superficial adoration from others. It convinces you that if you can achieve these things, you will feel powerful, whole, and complete. However, with every new acquisition and each new like or follow on social media, it is never enough. Like the mythical figure who ate fruit only to become hungrier with every bite, you also feel increasingly empty and lost.

Today, the Distractor is more powerful than ever, tempting you with quick fixes and overwhelming you with an excess of information and false promises. It suggests that you can buy happiness and that a sense of fulfillment is just one "click" away. This is how the Distractor diverts your attention from what will truly help you. Neglecting or misusing your creativity for superficial distractions is one of its primary goals. The Distractor's grand strategy is to drain your creative energy and motivation. Easy, quick answers are the name of the game, but they keep you from reaching your full potential. Over time, this leaves you uninspired and unmotivated. As you have fewer achievements to actually take pride in, the Distractor's message that you have nothing to offer the world becomes reinforced.

The Distractor's Traps

The Distractor lures you with quick fixes and easy rewards—whether it's materialism, social validation, shortcuts in academics, or chasing trends. Each of the traps listed below are ways the

Distractor diverts your energy away from meaningful growth, leaving you stuck in a cycle of fleeting satisfaction and disconnection.

Validation through social media. Imagine a teenager scrolling through social media, seeking validation through likes and comments. The Distractor whispers, "Just one more like, one more comment, and you'll finally feel accomplished." Despite accumulating likes and comments, the feeling of emptiness grows as each notification serves as a temporary distraction from deeper, unresolved feelings of inadequacy.

Materialism and consumption. Picture a high school student constantly striving to acquire the latest gadgets and fashion items, believing that each new purchase will bring lasting happiness. The Distractor convinces them that their worth is tied to their possessions. Yet, the initial excitement quickly fades, leaving them feeling more disconnected and unfulfilled with each purchase.

Shortcuts in academics. Consider a student who is constantly seeking shortcuts in their homework, opting for quick fixes to get through their reading and paperwork over thorough understanding of the material they're supposed to be learning. The Distractor tempts them with the promise of efficiency, saying, "Just get it done quickly, it really doesn't matter anyway." As a result, the student produces subpar work, missing opportunities to develop their skills and failing to take pride in their accomplishments. Over time, their lack of deep engagement with their tasks leads to feelings of incompetence and dissatisfaction.

Creativity and passing trends. Think of a teenager who once found joy in drawing intricate designs but now spends hours mindlessly browsing through art trends online. The Distractor tells them, "Your ideas are only valuable if they fit the trend." They abandon their unique style in favor of imitating popular art, losing their creative spark. As their originality fades, so does their passion, leaving them feeling creatively drained and uninspired.

Breaking the Cycle of Instant Gratification

As the Mastermind, you understand that the essence of self-satisfaction often comes from your ability to create, build, and see through the completion of your projects—a domain where the Wizard thrives. By steering you away from these rewarding activities, the Distractor deprives you of the satisfaction that comes from true achievement and self-driven success. This theft of opportunity not only diminishes your sense of accomplishment but also erodes your belief in your own capabilities.

In today's fast-paced world, where efficiency and constant activity are highly valued, the Distractor finds fertile ground. The push for quicker solutions and the constant stream of distractions can overwhelm and paralyze your thought processes. Even the very tools designed to enhance your productivity and connectivity can lead you into a pattern of superficial engagement with ideas. This will reduce your ability to handle challenges independently over time.

Lack of deep engagement with your activities initiates a cycle of chasing instant gratification in which the Distractor continues to flourish. To break this cycle of avoiding challenges followed by seeking quick rewards, followed by more avoidance and quick rewards, you need to resist the allure of the easy way out and make a deliberate effort to engage deeply with your tasks. This is how you reclaim your internal Wizard's power to transform challenges into opportunities for growth.

Wizard Training

Harnessing the power of the Wizard within you is crucial for being successful in life. The following exercises, which are straightforward and can be easily integrated into your daily routine, are designed to help you develop your capacity for focus, creativity, and resilience. By strengthening these natural abilities, you will become more able to stay engaged with meaningful tasks and unlock new levels of creative talent and dormant ability.

Exercise 1: Self-Expression Journal

The objective of writing a self-expression journal is to enhance your creativity and self-expression. This daily practice will encourage you to explore your thoughts and emotions without fear of judgment. It can boost your overall sense of well-being and ignite your imagination.

Instructions. Dedicate just fifteen minutes a day to writing, drawing, or doodling in a journal at a time of your choosing. As you doodle, let your thoughts flow freely without censorship or self-criticism. Once a week, reflect on your entries to assess your progress and notice any emerging patterns.

What can you expect? Over time, you'll notice an increase in your ability to express yourself and a greater sense of freedom in your creative endeavors. Patience is key, so remind yourself periodically that your ideas and creations will evolve gradually.

Exercise 2: Digital Detox Hours

Constant digital engagement can fragment your attention and sap your creative energy. Taking regular breaks from screens helps us reconnect with our thoughts and the world around us, fostering deeper focus and inspiration. The objective of reducing digital distractions for defined periods is to enhance our ability to focus for longer and longer stretches of time.

Instructions. Set specific hours each day when you avoid using digital devices. For example, your rule might be "No screens between 3 PM and 5 PM" (the time when you usually do your homework), or "No screens after 8 PM" (which is close to the time you need to get to sleep).

During your screen-free period, engage in offline activities like reading, drawing, doing homework, or spending time outdoors. A "detox" done in the evening will help you wind down before bed and improve your focus.

Gradually increase the duration of your digital detox.

What can you expect? Initially, you may find it challenging to disconnect from your electronic devices, but then, over time, you'll begin to experience a sense of calm and improved concentration when you do a "detox." Your creativity will flourish as your mind becomes less cluttered with digital noise.

Exercise 3: Hidden Abilities

Trying new activities can reveal our hidden talents and interests. This exercise will encourage you to step out of your comfort zone, see if activities you normally dismiss are better than you imagined, and help you potentially discover new passions, which can invigorate your creativity and provide a sense of accomplishment. The objective is to nurture dormant talents. Don't be afraid to play, have fun, and experiment with ideas regardless of the outcome!

Instructions. Choose an activity to try out that interests you, but which you've never tried before (for example, singing, painting, playing a musical instrument, or creative writing). Dedicate at least thirty minutes a few days a week to practicing and exploring this new hobby.

Let's say that you've always been curious about photography. There's a camera in your phone or someone is willing to lend you a camera, so you don't need to buy any special equipment. You will dedicate an hour after school in the afternoon walking around your neighborhood taking pictures. You might also make a special trip to the library to find books on special photography techniques and watch some videos on YouTube discussing concepts like framing an image, playing with contrasting colors, and capturing action. The idea, in this case, would be to bring your unique perception of the world to your exploration of the images you make.

As you explore the activity, keep a journal of your experiences and progress over the span of a month. In the photography example, after taking your photos, you will write about your experiences and what you've discovered in your journal.

What can you expect? As you explore new hobbies, you'll discover new facets of your creativity. Be patient. Skills develop with time and practice, and the journey of learning is as valuable as the results.

Exercise 4: Flow State Activities

The flow state is when we are so fully absorbed in an activity, often leading to high levels of creativity and productivity. This exercise helps you identify and cultivate activities that bring you into this optimal state. This state is created when we are challenged, albeit not overwhelmed, and we are intently focused on what we're doing.

The objective of this exercise is simply to engage in activities that naturally lead you into a state of flow.

Instructions. Identify an activity that you enjoy which challenges you enough to keep you fully engaged (for example, playing a musical instrument, coding, or playing Ultimate Frisbee). Schedule regular times to do this activity without interruption.

Notice and reflect on the conditions that helped you enter the flow state (if and when it occurred) afterward. If it helps you could write about it in your journal to remind yourself in the future.

Maybe you love playing the guitar. Set aside time each week to practice more challenging pieces. Pay attention to how you feel when you get fully immersed in your playing and lose track of time. Entering a state of flow, which feels blissful, is not something that happens at our command. It is like a "gift from the gods" of old, a fortunate happenstance. But you can get better at creating conditions that lead you to flow. Just be patient as you explore and refine the conditions that best help you enter flow. After you do enter a flow state, you will notice how it can significantly enhance your creativity and satisfaction.

BY ENGAGING IN these exercises, you'll cultivate the Wizard's innate powers and abilities, enhancing focus, creativity, and resilience. Keep in mind that these exercises are tools for your growth. Feel free to choose those to do that resonate most with you at any given moment. Over time, you may find that certain exercises were more beneficial or relevant to your needs than others. You can always return to the other exercises later on. Remember, progress takes patience—allow your ideas, transformations, and creations to unfold naturally.

Final Thoughts on the Wizard

In your journey of personal growth and development, the Wizard is your innate capacity for creativity, innovation, and visionary thinking. A force of nature, the Wizard has propelled humanity from basic survival to the exploration of the cosmos through groundbreaking inventions like fire, the wheel, and written language. This same transformative power resides within you, enabling you to envision, create, and bring your dreams to fruition.

To harness this power, it is crucial to clear your mind of the constant noise and pressures of modern life. By engaging in practices that promote stillness and mindfulness, you create mental space where new thoughts, insights, and creative ideas can flourish. This process revitalizes the Wizard within you, offering a clearer, more inspired view of the world.

The Wizard's ability to transform challenges into opportunities and bring innovative solutions to life is essential for your personal fulfillment and success. However, this potential is often hindered by the presence of the Distractor—a force within you that diverts your attention and energy toward trivial and distressing matters. The Distractor promotes false beliefs in dependency, conformity, and scarcity, leading to a cycle of unfulfilled desires and missed opportunities.

Engaging in exercises that nurture creativity, focus, and deep concentration is vital for unlocking the Wizard's full potential. By recognizing and resisting the Distractor's influence, you can reclaim your creative power and direct it toward meaningful and productive pursuits. These practices will help you stay engaged with your tasks, manage distractions, and cultivate a mindset of growth and resilience.

Looking ahead, your journey of nurturing the Wizard will involve ongoing commitment to your personal growth and self-discovery. Here are five keys to making the journey a success.

Key 1: Consistent practice. Regular engagement in mindfulness and creative exercises will strengthen the Wizard's capabilities.

Consistency is key to developing deeper focus, enhancing creativity, and building resilience.

Key 2: *Mindful reflection.* Periodic reflection on your progress and experiences will provide valuable insights and guide adjustments in your practices. This reflection fosters self-awareness and continuous improvement.

Key 3: *Adapting to challenges.* As challenges arise, your innovative thinking and problem-solving skills will be crucial. Embracing a flexible and adaptive mindset will help you navigate uncertainties and leverage opportunities for growth.

Key 4: *Cultivating a supportive environment.* Surrounding yourself with supportive and like-minded individuals can amplify the Wizard's influence. Collaborative efforts and shared experiences can inspire and motivate continued personal development.

Key 5: *Limiting digital engagement.* In an increasingly digitized world, finding a balance between online and offline activities will be essential. Reducing digital distractions and prioritizing meaningful engagements will enhance your focus and creativity.

By embracing these keys, you can fully activate the Wizard in you, transforming your life into a continuous journey of exploration, innovation, and fulfillment. As you move forward, the Wizard's visionary power will guide you toward realizing your highest potential and contributing positively to the world around you.

CHAPTER FOUR

....

THE LOVER

Have you ever wondered why love is so important to feeling truly happy? Being loved and loving others is essential to a fulfilling life. Love is a complex and multifaceted emotion that involves deep affection, care, and attachment. It provides us with emotional connection, compassion, commitment, acceptance, selflessness, and joy. Human connection is vital for our well-being, offering a sense of belonging, security, and happiness. This is true for children, teens, and adults alike. Love sustains us, gives us comfort in a difficult world, and helps us know that we are okay and not alone. When we love others and are loved in return, it reinforces that we are part of something bigger, such as a family, a community, or a one-on-one shared human experience. We love others because they are like us, and we are like them, part of the same family.

Consider Liam, surrounded by his relatives at a backyard cookout in August. Their knowledge and appreciation of him filled him with a sense of calm, bliss, and security. He never wanted the cookouts to end when the cold weather arrived. The laughter, the shared stories, and the unconditional love he felt in those moments created a sanctuary for him. This love and connection provided Liam with the comfort and assurance that he was valued and not alone, illustrating the profound importance of love in our lives. When he was a youngster he would run to greet relatives who came to his family's home by throwing his arms around their legs. It made them feel great when this little boy openly displayed his affection for them.

Similarly, from an early age Charlotte's parents loved adventuring with their daughter, doing their best to keep up with her endless questions and sharing her excitement about nature. Their love and involvement in her life provided her with a sense of security and joy, through her adolescence, always showing her that she was cherished and never alone. They felt rewarded by the love she returned to them as well, which she demonstrated by making collages out of flowers and bringing home pretty pebbles, shells, and pieces of driftwood she picked up while hiking near the shore.

Both Liam and Charlotte's experiences demonstrate how love is crucial for children, teens, and adults. It sustains us, offers comfort, and helps us understand that we are valued and connected. Love, in all its forms, creates a foundation of support and happiness that allows us to thrive and find fulfillment in our lives.

Charlotte's explorations taught her valuable lessons. She learned to appreciate the small wonders of life and find joy in everyday things. She developed a deep curiosity about the world. The more she experienced these natural wonders, the more alive and part of something bigger than herself she felt.

Charlotte and her parents dreamed of making a difference in the world through their discoveries in the natural world, fostering a sense of interconnectedness with all living things. Shared experiences, collaborative fun, and taking on challenges together for the welfare of their community deepened their bond and love.

These joint experiences reinforced the bond between Charlotte and her parents. For example, during a plane trip, they would marvel at the clouds and tiny cars below. On road trips, they would play games spotting interesting sights. These shared activities helped Charlotte learn to see adults as helpful and caring, a perspective that transferred to other important adults at school and in her community.

As Charlotte grew older, she started noticing a new kind of feeling—something more complex than her love for the grass waving in the wind or the thrill of finding a new pebble on a hike. This feeling was tied to people, particularly to one person she met recently, and it left her feeling giddy, nervous, and filled with an unexplainable excitement. Was this love? Or something else?

We often use the term *falling in love* to describe the sensation of being intensely drawn to someone. But there's a distinction between true love and infatuation. Infatuation is like a bright, sudden spark that consumes your attention—powerful, but often temporary. It's when you feel butterflies in your stomach, can't stop thinking about a person, and see them as perfect, even if you barely know them. This stage of initial attraction can be thrilling but it is usually based on fantasy rather than reality.

Love, on the other hand, grows over time. It's not just about the excitement or thrill of being around someone; it's about truly knowing, accepting, and valuing the other person for who they are, flaws and all. Love is built on trust, respect, and shared experiences. It involves a deeper connection and a willingness to support each other, even when things aren't easy.

Charlotte's first experience of infatuation was exciting, but it also taught her some difficult and important lessons. She found herself constantly trying to impress the person she liked, often putting his needs above her own. One day, she realized she was spending so much time worrying about what he thought of her that she started losing touch with her own interests. She felt drained and confused because she had ignored her needs in an attempt to be what she thought this person wanted.

With the support of her parents and friends, Charlotte learned how part of building healthy relationships is maintaining her sense of self and respecting her own boundaries. It wasn't about changing who she was to fit someone else's expectations but being authentic and true to herself. This understanding allowed her to recognize when someone appreciated her for who she was versus when they were more interested in who they wanted her to be.

An illustration of this lesson would show Charlotte sitting in a garden with a tall fence around it, representing her personal boundaries. Inside the garden, flowers of different colors bloom, each representing her unique interests, values, and strengths. Only people who respect her garden—without trying to pluck her flowers or trample her grass—are welcome inside. Those who want to take more than they give or who disregard her boundaries are gently kept outside the fence.

Another important lesson Charlotte learned was the value of honesty—not just with others, but with herself. It's easy to convince ourselves that everything is fine in a relationship just because we want it to be. But being honest means acknowledging when something doesn't feel right, even if it's hard to admit. True love, whether it's romantic or platonic, is built on trust and open communication. It's about being able to say, "This is what I need" and "This is how I feel" without fear of judgment.

Charlotte spoke with a close friend about her mixed emotions after realizing that her crush wasn't treating her with the same respect she was giving him. Her friend listened, wisely only offering support, not solutions, which helped Charlotte see that honesty is the foundation of understanding and growth, both in herself and in her relationships.

Romantic interests, falling in love, and experiencing infatuation are all natural parts of growing up. What's important is learning to navigate these emotions with a sense of balance, self-respect, and honesty. It's okay to feel intense emotions, but it's equally important to stay grounded, know your boundaries, and recognize when a relationship is—or isn't—healthy for you.

Charlotte's journey into understanding love didn't stop at infatuation. It evolved into a deeper understanding of herself and what it means to be in a meaningful relationship. She discovered that love isn't just about excitement or being around someone who makes your heart race—it's about being with someone who sees and appreciates your true self, just like her parents did when she was a little girl exploring the grass and finding joy in the simple things.

With these lessons, Charlotte grew into a young woman who could embrace love and relationships with openness and confidence. She didn't need to chase after people who didn't appreciate her for who she was. Instead, she focused on building connections with those who valued and respected her boundaries, making each relationship a reflection of the love she held for herself.

The Lover Today

As Charlotte has gotten older, her relationships have become more virtual. She finds herself entering a world increasingly dominated by digital communication, leading to significant differences in the kind and quality of her connections compared to when she was younger. For one, in the kind of online interactions that are now routine in her life she often misses the nonverbal cues that are crucial for understanding others and adjusts her own behaviors to fit the people and circumstances she finds herself in. Without the ability to read body language, tone of voice, and facial expressions, it is harder for her to fully understand and connect with others.

This unsynchronized interaction, where individuals are not fully in tune with each other, can hinder the development of social skills and emotional intelligence.

By contrast, synchronized interactions involve a natural flow of communication, where participants are attuned to each other's cues and rhythms, fostering deeper understanding and connection.

Living out of sync, feeling out of sync, thinking you are not okay—these experiences are increasingly common for many young people. Over time, the nature of online interactions begins to take its toll. The lack of nonverbal cues makes it difficult to fully understand others, leading to miscommunication and misunderstanding. Without the ability to read body language, tone of voice, and facial expression, you miss out on the depth of human connection that fosters true understanding and empathy. This can leave you feeling isolated and disconnected, even when you're constantly "connected" through your devices. It's like everyone is alone all together.

The anonymity of the internet can also bring out the worst in people, exposing you to harsh criticisms, trolling, and cyberbullying. These negative experiences can make you more cautious and less willing to share your true self, for fear of being judged or ridiculed. As a result, you become more guarded, choosing to hide behind a carefully curated online persona rather than being open and authentic.

Over time, the love of many young people for the world fades. What was once new and exciting becomes old and familiar. You start to see more nuances and complexities in the world, recognizing areas where uncertainty and potential danger can exist. With age, your awareness changes. You shift from always being on the lookout for fun things to learn and explore to being on the lookout for the threat of embarrassment, rejection, and failure. The awe and wonder are gradually replaced by worries about safety, stability, and avoiding risks.

It's like going from "I can't wait, a new adventure!" to "You want me to do what? There's no way I can do that!" Initial excitement and curiosity are replaced by hesitation and fear. Suddenly, you're more focused on avoiding a metaphorical banana peel rather than wondering how it got there in the first place. This shift in perspective can lead to a more cautious and risk-averse approach to life, where the goal is to avoid discomfort and potential harm rather than seeking out new experiences and embracing the unknown.

In essence, the transition from an open, receptive, and spontaneous outlook to a fearful, guarded, and apprehensive one is a gradual process influenced by the nature of our complicated world today.

Your love affair with the world and the lessons you learn from it will be deeply rooted in your social interactions and relationships. Your early experiences will help determine how you look at the world. As you smell the flowers, watch the butterflies, pet dogs, and jump into swimming pools, you learn how things feel and how they respond to you. You learn in real-time and through feedback.

For an analogy, think of the game of tennis. Pickleball will suffice, too, if that is what you are into. When you play, you not only figure out how the ball bounces on the court, the weight of the racquet in your hand, and the amount of force needed to get the ball back over the net and in the place that you want it to land.

Well, this kind of information represents just a fraction of what you are learning every day as you move through the world.

From experience, you are learning how well your body coordinates itself, how your eyes and hands work together, what it's like to work through frustration, how to handle making mistakes when there's an audience, and so much more. In racquet sports, you pay attention to the tendencies of your opponents, such as what moves they like to make, if they over rely on shots from the right or left, if receiving your shot is harder for them from different angles, and so on. This learning does not take place outside of a relationship. Social learning, attunement, give and take, and a sense of belonging are all integral to this process. When with others, you are constantly tuning in to their cues and adjusting your actions to fit the moment. This attunement helps you understand and anticipate others' moves and time your actions with theirs.

In social settings beyond physical activities, you also learn the unspoken rules of interaction: how to read emotions, respond to social cues, and navigate complex social dynamics. This social learning is crucial for developing a sense of belonging and forming your identity within a community.

Culture and identity are deeply intertwined with social experiences. The way you engage with the world, the activities you participate in, and the relationships you form all contribute to your cultural identity. Through these interactions, you learn the values, norms, and behaviors of your community, which help shape your sense of self.

Being in sync with others fosters a sense of belonging, making you feel connected and understood. It helps you build relationships and develop a strong sense of community that gives you purpose and meaning. These relationships along with their shared experiences are essential for social cohesion and personal well-being.

While your love for the world can fade as you mature, it is never really gone. There is a Lover deep within you—the part of you that is all about savoring and basking in the richness of life. This part of you nurtures and sustains you, gravitating to beauty like a bee to honey, and it understands the interconnectedness of all things.

We are all connected in profound ways, bound by the invisible threads of our shared humanity and experiences. The Lover has a deep appreciation for this fact, recognizing how our actions, emotions, and lives intertwine with those of others. In many ways, that innocent kid in love with the world is still inside you, feeling the deep sense of interconnectedness with everything around them. Sure, you have grown, and your tastes have changed, but there is always so much more in this world to experience and love. The world is a vast and diverse place, waiting for you to discover its features and potential.

The Lover in you never really goes away; it can, however, fall into a kind of deep sleep. Like a bear in the winter, choosing to hibernate until the warmth of spring returns. The Lover can also go into hiding when the world seems too cold and harsh.

There is tremendous creative and healing power in life. It can be hard to see sometimes, but moments that will fill your heart with gratitude and awe are out there waiting. You simply have to step into them. A breathtaking sunset, tranquil countryside, or a quiet snowy morning haven't disappeared from the planet, no matter how hard things can seem. Life gets so busy, we can get so distracted that we forget to stop and smell the roses, so to speak. We neglect the power of just having a delicious meal, or the rejuvenation that comes from a warm hug.

I sometimes like to watch my dog play with a bone or her squeaky toy. We adopted Minji from an elderly couple that couldn't care for her the way she needed anymore. Being two young parents with two young children who desperately also wanted a little pooch, we jumped at the chance. It helped that she is a gorgeous, sweet, little mammal with only patience and love in her heart.

Watching Minji is a lesson in meditation. She is in the moment, present, without a past or a future to worry or interrupt her chewing, pawing, and licking. It's a model for how to be. We all need these reminders. As I sit listening to her teeth scrape the bone she's wrestling over, I can feel my blood pressure drop, my mind begins to clear, and a smile creep onto to my face. Her blissful ignorance of anything on either side of the moment is mesmerizing.

Like a playful puppy, the Lover in you also wants to remind you to stop, take a deep breath, and notice the beauty around you. To bask in the calm that comes simply from being in the ordinariness of the day. It's funny the things you start to notice when you are caught up in your own head, distracted by worries, and your mood hijacked by something you have no control over. These are often the times when I find it easiest to connect with others. Sometimes it's a cashier in the supermarket, a person waiting in line, or someone sitting next to you on the bus. These small, spontaneous interactions can bring back a sense of connection and remind you of the importance of being present and open to the world around you.

Relationships Prior to Adulthood

All of us learn the most about love in our earliest relationships—even if what we learn is not particularly healthy for us. At home with our families, we practice loving others and experiencing what it is like to be loved as well. Parents, siblings, and caregivers are our first teachers, providing us with lessons in trust, understanding, and closeness.

In time, you'll internalize the lessons from your early relationships with family and friends, and in your first romantic encounters, and these folks will contribute to the foundation of your self-understanding and lovability that you build.

As you ventured into the world of school and friendships as a younger child, you used the earliest models of relationships to help you. Equipped with invaluable skills picked up from interacting with your siblings and classmates, you were then given a choice year after year over the friendships you would maintain. In the future, they will help you articulate for yourself how you want to build an extended family (to go with your inherited family). Often teens like you spend so much time with their same-age friends that their friends are their brothers and sisters for all intents and purposes. Peers are important.

To flesh out our ideas about relationships a bit, let's take a look at some everyday examples of how they may influence you.

Friendships. If you grew up surrounded by supportive and empathetic family members, you likely approach conflicts with friends with understanding and a willingness to resolve issues. You have seen firsthand how this works, and the good it does. So, you internalize the model.

By contrast, if you grew up needing to fend for yourself, you might approach conflicts with friends defensively or try to avoid them. You may have learned that differences of opinion create anger and resentment, and can lead others to try to impose their views on you. So, you get ready for battle each time you sense a difference of opinion. Thankfully, you can change this way of doing business. First, you need to experience the alternative.

Managing anxiety and stress. If your parents provided reassurance and love, you learned that seeking support from others was okay to do and would help you cope with and get through stressful times. In fact, you may be drawn to, and make friends with, people like your family in how they cope in life. This can be a very good thing when these early people were good influences.

Sometimes early experiences can lead us away from others when we are stressed. You might have learned to handle anxiety and stress on your own and now cope with these things by withdrawing or using strategies that lead to isolation. For example, isolation by scrolling on social media or gaming excessively. You might also comfort yourself by eating or drinking things that make you feel good in the moment, instead of reaching out to others for support, even though these choices may not be the best for your physical or emotional health.

Romantic relationships. The same dynamics hold in close relationships. If you grew up in a home where affection and love were freely given, it will be easier to express your feelings and needs when you find yourself in a romantic relationship than if you did not receive affection and support. This is because your feelings were accepted, which taught you they are okay to have, and part of what make you a healthy person.

On the flip side, when empathy and affection are scarce, kids learn that their feelings are not very important. If this was the case in your home, then you may have learned to anticipate rejection, so distancing yourself from others seems like a sensible strategy to avoid pain.

The good news is that no matter whether your experiences have been good, bad, or so-so, you can have the capacity to grow emotionally and socially. This means you can build strong, supportive relationships in your life today. These types of relationships can be invaluable to deal with all the weirdness that comes with being a teen and preparing yourself to handle the demands of adulthood.

Personality Masks

To truly open up and connect with others, you have to learn to drop the masks you wear each day. I'm not talking about Halloween masks. I mean the false personalities that we, as people, get really good at creating to help us get through life when we feel vulnerable. These masks are designed to get others to love and be affectionate toward us. We sometimes say what we think other people want to hear and adopt a vocabulary that gets positive reactions from them, for instance. The problem is, the mask isn't who we are, so masking our genuine thoughts and feelings really winds up cutting us off from establishing true connection in our relationships.

A lot of times, people—of all ages, not only young people—hide behind a masks for fear that who they really are is not good enough. They fear that if others really find out about the mean, ugly thoughts they think or the moments of anger and irrationality they feel, people wouldn't be able to stand being around them. Except, everyone has such parts in them. Sadly, you'll never really get to learn this if you choose to put on masks that you believe others will be attracted to, playing roles instead of being yourself.

Let's look at someone we will call Jake. He grew up in a small, rural town in the South. His parents then relocated his family when they sold their farm. They moved to a big city in the Midwest, where Jake became a new kid at the local middle school. Afraid that the other kids would make fun of him for being a "hillbilly" or a "dumb country boy," he decided to create a mask for himself. Previously, Jake always wore jeans and tee-shirts with his trusty work boots, but now he swapped them for the latest sneakers and trendy urban-style outfits. He hid his Southern drawl, practicing speaking in a more neutral tone every night before bed, even though it made him feel like he was losing a part of himself.

Jake loved talking about his adventures in the countryside, riding horses, fishing in a creek, and exploring the woods with his dog, Gunnar. But at his new school, he kept these stories to himself. He didn't want to risk being teased and laughed at. Instead, to fit in, he spoke about video games he didn't really play and music he didn't actually enjoy hearing. He tried to act tough, even laughing along with jokes he found hurtful and rude. As he did all of this, Jake felt a growing sense of isolation. The mask he had made was becoming a barrier between him and his new friends. It also started to block him off from important parts of himself.

One day, during lunch, Jake overheard a group of kids talking about their weekend plans. One boy, Sam, mentioned going camping with his family. Jake's eyes lit up, but he hesitated to respond. Sam noticed the reaction, however, and asked if Jake liked camping. Tentatively, Jake shared a bit about his love for the outdoors, expecting the worst. To his surprise, Sam and the others listened to what he said with interest, asking questions and sharing their own stories.

Encouraged by the other boys' reactions, Jake slowly began to open up more to them. He told them about Gunnar and the fishing trips with his grandpa. He shared tales about the peaceful nights he'd spent in a sleeping bag lying under the stars gazing at a sky free from the city's bright lights and noise. Against his expectations, Sam and the others don't laugh or scoff; they were actually fascinated.

As Jake started to realize that his new friends could appreciate him for who he really was, he began to drop the mask, letting his true self be known. As Jake became more comfortable in his own skin, he learned that being different wasn't something to be ashamed of. Rather, it was part of what made him interesting to others and could be celebrated.

Jake fell into the trap of creating a People-pleaser mask. This type of mask drives you to prioritize others' approval more than your own needs and desires. The trouble with maintaining this façade is that you must constantly do more to earn their respect and acceptance.

There are many kinds of masks you can make to hide behind. For instance, another common mask, the Comedian, means using humor to deflect serious conversations so you can avoid confronting strong, unpleasant emotions. When you act as the Comedian, you hide your true feelings and see them as liabilities. You laugh even when you want to cry, joke even when life hands you disappointment.

Don't get me wrong, a sense of humor is an excellent way to cope with life. Personally, I love to laugh and use humor all the time in my conversations. But if humor becomes your only way of dealing with life, then you might have a problem. That is what wearing a mask does—it covers everything up. If you aren't careful, it can wind up suffocating the real you, depriving you of the "oxygen" that comes from authentic connections with others.

Another mask is the Caregiver. This one involves prioritizing the well-being of others to the extent that you neglect your own needs. While it shares similarities with the People-pleaser mask, the

Caregiver mask is about feeling responsible for others, more than it is about seeking approval or validation.

Then there are the Overachiever and the Perfectionist, two similar masks that will push you to seek success and validation through accomplishment while hiding feelings of inadequacy and fear of being judged.

The thing to remember is not the name of the mask but the fact that all masks are traps. They are traps because they promise you love and acceptance but leave you doubting the love you receive once you get it. You doubt it because you know it could be the mask that people love, not necessarily you. Or at least that is what your brain tells you.

If someone doesn't know the genuine you "warts and all," as the old expression goes, then it becomes much more difficult to feel truly loved by them. This is why dropping these masks is so important.

Now, let's apply this concept to the online world, where creating a false self or personal brand is often encouraged. Although putting on a mask in person brings its own challenges, the online environment presents unique issues of its own. When we engage with social media, we often curate our profiles to show the best, most appealing versions of ourselves. We post pictures that highlight our successes, filtering out our imperfections, and craft updates that reflect a life of constant excitement and positivity. This online persona becomes a digital mask, one designed specifically to attract likes, comments, and followers. But it's an idealized version of someone we wish to be seen as, not the person we truly are.

Imagine that your online persona portrays you as always happy, always successful, and always in control. The people who follow you may admire this image, but they are admiring a facade. When you interact with others through this persona, you might get positive feedback and validation from your followers/connections, but those reactions are based on this version of yourself that you yourself know isn't entirely real. This can lead to you to feel feelings of loneliness and isolation because the connections you have are made through the mask. Those "friends" are not interacting with your true self.

Over time, maintaining this persona could be exhausting. You might find yourself constantly worrying about how you're being perceived or to spend hours curating new content and feeling anxious about whether you're living up to the image you've created. The more you invest in the success of this false self, the more you can lose touch with who you really are. Such a disconnect can lead sooner or later to a sense of emptiness and loneliness. Deep down, you recognize that your relationships and interactions aren't built on your authentic self. Yet, you genuinely want your true self to be accepted and loved.

Your True Self

When you hide your true self from the world, you deny the world the special qualities you have to offer. Also, there are sometimes parts of ourselves we want to disown when we're young that end up being important to us or valuable in a certain context later in our lives.

Putting on a mask is like using a cover stick to hide a pimple. When you try to paint over a blemish with makeup, it doesn't mean the blemish is gone. It is just covered up. The same goes for your personality. Your least favorite parts of yourself are still there. Only, unlike a blemish on your face, these parts are neglected versions of you.

Here's the problem: No one likes being ignored, especially these neglected parts of you.

Psychologically, a lot of us spend too much time trying to be someone we are not. We don't like our names, the color of our hair, how much we talk, or how much we weight. That takes a lot of energy! Imagine how you would be freed up without all those worries. We scrutinize our bodies, picking out our perceived imperfections and wishing we could be like the people we see in the movies. So we get haircuts, go on diets, and buy all kinds of cosmetics—all in the hope of escaping our flaws. It's an internal drama.

For example, have you ever felt like if you could only lose a few pounds, be a couple inches taller, less emotional, or sound smarter, then maybe you could finally leave behind that weird, awkward kid you used to be—or at least felt like you were?

I hear about this so often in my practice: People try to make themselves into some new version of themselves. They are not as interested—at first—in learning to love who they are as they are in trying to get rid of the qualities they don't like. But almost always, without except these kinds of "makeovers" are doomed.

Why? Put simply, the focus is on the wrong thing. It's like paying attention to how oddly you think your face is shaped, instead of appreciating how beautifully you listen to and empathize with your friends. It means you're failing to see what draws people to you. Which is to say that you already have things about you that are beloved.

Still, you worry this isn't enough. So, you continue to worry about being cool, making a name for yourself, and being liked by people you probably wouldn't want to hang out with in the first place if you were being truthful. You fear others will see the real "ugly" you, instead of realizing that the real weirdo, nerd, spaz, space cadet, goofy side of you is what others like. When you let this side out for others to see, it makes them feel okay to reveal more of themselves in return. You help them feel less alone in the world.

When it comes down to it, you are a wonder of nature. It is true. Like the intricate patterns in a leaf, the plumage of a bird, or the striations found in granite mountains, nature has made its mark on you. Of course, you won't sprout wings and fly, or anything. Sorry, as much as I wish it to be true, we humans still must rely on our inventions for that. But, just as a tree fights to branch out and get all the nutrients it needs for life, you've been given specific qualities that will help you thrive. The more you accept these qualities, and the more able you are to leverage them, the more capable and in charge of your destiny you will become.

Like a river that has the innate power to carve its path across the landscape, you too are able innately to carve out a path for yourself.

Imagine going through life feeling invisible, with no one noticing or caring about you. It would be like being in an emotional desert, making you desperately thirsty for even the slightest bit of kindness. You might then tolerate disrespectful behavior more than you should or let others take advantage of your good nature, believing you must take what you can get.

If you suspect that this may be what you are doing, then I invite you to consider that everyone needs love, just like they need food, water, and air. It is a basic necessity. But you do not have to tolerate any kind of mistreatment in order to be loved. When you learn to accept and love all of who you are, you become stronger as a whole person. You become a person who can then love others fearlessly, and help them do the same for themselves. You also learn when to walk away from relationships that are not healthy for you.

The Splitter

While you need love from others, you also have a set of self-protection instincts designed to shield you from those acting in bad faith, trying to exploit or take advantage of your loving nature. This self-preservation instinct kicks in mainly during social situations. For example, when you feel judged or criticized in a group, your instinct might urge you to withdraw to protect your feelings. If you sense rejection, you might preemptively distance yourself to avoid further pain. This instinct is a primal survival mechanism meant to shield you from emotional harm.

Just as there is a yin quality that complements each yang quality in the world (a light for every darkness, a softness for every harshness), so there is for the Lover. The Splitter is the anti-Lover persona that arises from a twisted sense of self-preservation which is rooted in your primal survival instincts. It emerges from experiences of personal pain, sorrow, and resentment, feelings we all experience at one point or another and then spend most of our lives trying to avoid.

The Splitter sows division and distrust, magnifying minor misunderstandings and insecurities in our relationships. Trying to shut down the Lover in you, the Splitter promotes solitude as superiority and cynicism as wisdom. It tries to convince you that withdrawing from others is a form of strength and that mistrusting people is a sign of intelligence. All the while, the Splitter's aim is to detach you from your passions and interests, setting you on a path filled with loneliness instead of connection and joy.

As we have discussed, all of us now live in a technology-driven, online world that often feels disconnected from reality. Constantly being bom-barded with incomplete, biased, and incorrect information, which happens every day online, can leave you feeling disconnected, confused, and afraid. Social media and online sources of news often amplify these feelings by creating a sense of shallow connection because filtered and curated interactions lack the depth and authenticity of face-to-face communication. The feedback loop is distorted, with likes and comments replacing genuine, in-the-moment responses.

In this context, it's too easy to fall into the trap of forming in-group and out-group biases. Imagine you're in school and part of a popular friend group. *In-group bias* is when you favor and prioritize the interests, opinions, and members of your own friend group over those of other groups. For example, you favor acting over playing chess, debating over volleyball. This can look like giving more trust, praise, and support to your friends. Conversely, *out-group bias* is when you view people outside your group with suspicion, negativity, or hostility. This often leads to negative stereotypes and unfair treatment toward those who aren't part of your group.

Online platforms facilitate the formation of in-groups based on shared interests, beliefs, and identities. While these in-groups can provide a sense of belonging and support from likeminded individuals, they can also create echo chambers where only similar opinions are shared and reinforced. This limits exposure to diverse perspectives and critical thinking, contributing to a skewed understanding of reality. Moreover, those perceived as part of the out-group may face cyberbullying, exclusion, and negative stereotyping, leading to social isolation and distress. The anonymity and distance provided by the online world can exacerbate these behaviors, making it easier to dehumanize and mistreat others.

To navigate the complexities of in-group and out-group bias in the digital age, it is crucial that we develop awareness and educate ourselves on these dynamics. Recognizing the impact of in-group and out-group biases can help you understand and manage your interactions more effectively. It also helps to know what you are seeking when you go surfing online. Media literacy and critical thinking skills are essential in discerning the quality and reliability of online information, helping you avoid the pitfalls of misinformation and biased content—and random advice from strangers. Being mindful of these influences allows you to nurture the Lover within and maintain genuine connections in an increasingly digital world.

Imagine two friends, Emily and Sarah, who have always been close. One day, Emily texts Sarah about an important event in her life, but Sarah is busy with schoolwork and doesn't respond immediately. Emily starts to feel neglected and unimportant, thinking that Sarah doesn't care about her anymore. Meanwhile, Sarah, overwhelmed with her workload, feels guilty for not being able to respond to Emily as she would like.

This is where the Splitter steps in, magnifying the girls' minor misunderstandings. Emily begins to believe that Sarah's lack of response is a sign of deeper issues in their friendship, and she starts to pull away, thinking it's better to distance herself than to feel hurt. Sarah, sensing Emily's withdrawal but not understanding why it's happening, feels rejected and starts to think that maybe Emily doesn't value their friendship as much as she thought.

Both friends begin to isolate themselves from each other, influenced by the Splitter's whispers of cynicism and distrust. Instead of talking it out and reconnecting, they drift further apart, each thinking the worst of the other's intentions. Emily starts to immerse herself in solitary activities, convincing herself that she's better off alone, while Sarah becomes more engrossed in her schoolwork, believing that focusing on her studies is the only way to avoid the pain of rejection.

In reality, a simple conversation could have resolved the misunderstanding. By not allowing the Splitter to take hold, Emily and Sarah could have expressed their feelings and reaffirmed their bond. Emily, being new at these kinds of more mature relationships where people talk about their feelings, and what they think about each other, didn't have the experience or training to know what to do. First Emily started to recognize the Splitter's influence on her, and she started to challenge the negative thoughts. This gave her more confidence to approach Sara and check in to see if there was any truth to the faulty conclusions she was reaching.

Growing up and facing the world outside of your home, school, and community can be intimidating. Part of this feeling comes from the fact that there are so many things to learn and understand, making it feel like you have to master everything in a short period of time. The Splitter plays upon your fears, making it seem like you are all alone in this world. It convinces you that you can only rely on yourself and that, in the end, others will let you down and turn their backs on you when it really counts.

The more you drift from connecting with others, the more likely you are to live in an isolation of experiences that are crucial for your social and emotional health. Social media, text messages, and even video chatting don't compare to real-time give-and-take experiences where you see, hear, and feel understood and supported. Loneliness breeds distrust and hostility, making it harder to see the good in others and yourself.

As a person, you need human connection to be reminded there are people who can relate to your experiences—the good, the bad, and the ugly. They can also help you become stronger by providing comfort, advice, and understanding.

Like ivy that will gradually erode even the strongest brick building, the Splitter wants to break you down. It creeps and crawls, looking for little cracks it can sink its roots into, your tiny doubts and worries, seeing them as openings to pull and pry you away from others. As it does this, you begin to believe you are too different from everyone else; so no one could ever understand you, much less love you, completely.

To confuse you even more, the Splitter wants you to distrust your feelings when you have feelings of love. When we love someone or something, there's always a risk of suffering the pain of loss, disappointment, and rejection. The Splitter will try to convince you that the temporary nature of things makes them unworthy of any emotional investment. Why bother when everything just ends? "There is no point," it will say.

When this argument fails, the Splitter will convince you to try and control the outcome of things. Jealousy, envy, and possessiveness may start to influence your thoughts when the fear of loss and rejection begins to dominate your mindset. The Splitter tells you the more you give in to feelings of love, the more likely you are to be hurt.

The Splitter will repeat the following messages to you in your head over and over and in hundreds of different contexts.

"You are alone."

"No one understands you."

"If people really knew you, they would not like you."

"People only care about themselves."

"To be strong, you must do everything yourself."

"People will always disappoint, betray, or use you."

"Love always ends in loss and pain."

"If you really love something or someone you must possess it completely."

A World Divided

While smartphones offer numerous benefits in terms of connectivity and access to information, they also block you from real-time experiences. When you are in them, you reach for your device by reflex. When you feel lonely, instead of seeking others out, you pick up a phone or get on your laptop, only to magnify your feelings of sadness and the impression that you are left out. Research has shown that excessive screen time, particularly that which is spent on social media and video games, has been associated with issues like reduced physical activity, sleep disturbances, cyberbullying, and negative effects on mental health.

Amid these well-discussed concerns, there is another, often underestimated, yet profoundly significant aspect of life, which is being disrupted by technology's pervasive presence. Our days are filled with intermissions—our moments of rest from focusing on our daily activities—like letting our minds wander, greeting a friend, or chatting with the mail carrier dropping off a package. These moments are the pauses between our main tasks and activities— often called *liminal spaces* in design—the figurative waiting rooms, hallways, and entryways of life. These spaces in our daily schedule, which are times of transition, travel, and reflection, thread our days together, infusing them with a sense of camaraderie and shared humanity. The simple pleasure of catching up, sharing a laugh, engaging in friendly banter, or offering a helping hand to another person make our lives more meaningful and interesting. Even the seemingly mundane gesture of holding a door, giving directions to a stranger we'll never see again, or offering a genuine compliment on a stranger's choice of footwear make us feel rewarded by connection.

It is within these often understated spaces and fleeting moments, those we frequently take for granted or overlook, that we unearth hidden gems: humor that lifts the day, hope that sparks inspiration, refreshing pauses amid the rush, and the deep nourishment that comes from human connection. These in-between spaces provide a sanctuary where we find not only solace but also a profound sense of belonging.

Across various settings, the importance of these spaces in time is abundantly clear. In the professional world, research shows that good relationships at work help keep employees happy and loyal. In schools, these dynamics can make the difference between an enjoyable high school experience and a miserable one. Think about the casual chats in the hallways, the friendships built over lunch, or the random encounters on the way home. Even chance meetings at the local supermarket or at the movies can be meaningful. Together, these moments form the fabric of our social lives, turning everyday interactions into genuine connections.

As we navigate a world increasingly influenced by digital interactions, these in-between spaces are becoming more and more endangered. We need to appreciate how much these connections add to our lives—not just for the humor and lightness they bring, but for how they keep us grounded, strengthen our sense of community, and build the relationships that make life richer. The digital world may draw us in, but it's through our real-life connections that we find genuine understanding, support, and meaning.

Technology has subtly inserted itself into the fabric of these moments, changing how we think about and relate to each other. The casual chat at lunch might now be replaced by a flurry of digital messages, the lunch break companionship swapped for scrolling through social media feeds, and chance encounters overshadowed by the constant pull of our devices. While technology undoubtedly brings benefits and efficiencies, it can also distance us from the authenticity of human connection.

As technology continues to become more deeply woven into the fabric of our lives, it presents a mix of advantages and challenges, especially when it comes to developing social skills and strengthening family bonds. As technology seamlessly infiltrates the intimate moments of our daily existence, it positions itself as an intermediary, bridging the gap between us and our fellow human beings. The digital age promised greater interconnectedness, but it reveals a paradox: while genuine empathy and compassion should flourish, our ability to truly connect with others seems to fade.

Can a digital exchange ever take the place of the nuances of a face-to-face conversation? Can an emoji replace the warmth of a smile, or a text message convey the subtlest inflections of emotion?

The profound depth of understanding that can arise from a direct gaze, the reassurance that can be communicated by a friend's touch on our shoulder during a vulnerable moment, or the unspoken companionship found in the silence between words, these are the building blocks of genuine empathy and profound connection. While technology undoubtedly facilitates communication and fosters connections that transcend geographical boundaries, its true challenge lies in connecting others on a fundamentally human level.

A House Divided

The more the Splitter pushes you to seek external validation, the more you will lose sight of who you really are. In today's world, so much is built on external validation—likes, followers, grades, and praise. But in reality, you are much more than just your feelings, thoughts, and physical body. As a famous spiritual teacher once said: "You are the universe expressing itself as a human for a little while." Your worth doesn't come from achievements, looks, or what others think of you. Your true value is inside you and goes beyond the superficial.

It may take time, but to understand that your true value comes from within, rather than from the approval or praise of others, is one of the greatest gifts of this lifetime. Nineteenth-century Transcendentalist writer Ralph Waldo Emerson said it well: "To be yourself in a world that is constantly trying to make you something else is the greatest accomplishment."

The attention economy today places significant demands on you, gradually training you to seek validation and fulfillment outside yourself. Your focus is treated as a valuable commodity, with various online platforms and media constantly competing to capture and monetize your attention with catchy slogans, humor, pictures, and videos. And if you're not careful, this relentless competition for your attention could push you further away from recognizing your true worth, making it easy to lose sight of who you really are.

Take social media, for example. You might start off sharing photos or videos simply because it's fun or because you want to stay connected with friends. But over time, the number of likes, comments, and followers your posts receive becomes a measure of your self-worth. You begin posting content to get more engagement, to appear a certain way, or to avoid feeling left out. Instead of sharing your authentic self, you end up curating an image that you think others will approve of.

Similarly, you may find yourself joining clubs or taking on extracurricular activities because they look good on college applications—not because you're genuinely interested. Or maybe you push yourself to maintain a perfect GPA, not for your own satisfaction or love of learning, but to meet expectations set by your parents or teachers. In both cases, you're no longer doing these things for yourself but to earn external validation and approval.

Before long, you feel trapped in a cycle of constantly seeking recognition, checking and rechecking to ensure you're living up to others' standards. You do whatever you can to make people happy—without regard for the cost to your own well-being. This fear-driven approach might seem to work initially, boosting your productivity and earning accolades. But this approval is like sugar coating a toxic pill: it keeps you hooked, distracting you from your own needs and leading you to accept ideas and behaviors that ultimately undermine your sense of self.

Instead of helping, the relentless pursuit to prove your worth can actually backfire. Even when you're at the top—the star performer—you can always be replaced. There's always someone better, and this pressure erodes your self-esteem, warping your sense of judgment and leaving you feeling more inadequate and anxious. All the while, you are lovable just as you are.

Corporate America doesn't stand in the way of this kind of manipulation; it actively thrives on it. Corporations capitalize on making young people feel worried and scared of falling behind, missing out, being rejected, or ending up alone—so that you'll want to buy whatever "cure" they're selling.

While the Splitter tries to distract you with shallow temptations, the Lover is always there, talking to you, trying to redirect your attention and energy back toward things that resonate with you heart and spirit. You do not have to be alone, unless you choose to be, and the Lover is the part of you that wants to show you all the people and activities that are just waiting to lift you into a world filled with peace, joy, and human connection.

Lover Training

Think of emotional connections like sunlight to a plant. Being appreciated, respected, and surrounded by friends and family will recharge you and give you the strength to deal with challenges. These connections will nourish you, allowing you to grow and succeed. With this in mind, let's explore some behaviors to practice that will help you cultivate these vital connections.

Practicing love can be simpler than you might think. It's not all about flowers, Cupid, and boxes of candy. Sometimes, love is about small things, like really listening to someone. Try this the next time you are talking with someone: Make it your goal to understand what they're truly saying. Instead of just waiting for your turn to speak, focus on what they're sharing. Listen to their words, try to feel what they might be feeling, and watch their body language. Are they excited, worried, happy, or sad?

Exercise: Active Listening

Active listening is more than just hearing the words someone says. It's about really paying attention, understanding, and responding thoughtfully. When you actively listen, you show the person speaking that you genuinely care about what they're saying and that you're engaged in the conversation. By practicing these behaviors, you can strengthen your emotional connections, just like sunlight nourishes a plant, allowing both you and your relationships to thrive.

Here's how you can make active listening a part of your daily interactions.

Show you're engaged. When your friend is talking, put away your phone and make eye contact. Nod or give small verbal cues like "I see" or "That makes sense." This shows that you're focused on them and interested in what they have to say.

Reflect back what you hear. After they've said something important, repeat back what you've heard in your own words. For example, if your friend says they're stressed about an upcoming test, you might say, "So, you're feeling really anxious about the test on Friday?" This helps clarify their feelings and shows you're paying attention.

Ask questions. If you're not sure about something they said, ask for more details. Questions like "Can you tell me more about that?" or "What do you mean when you say . . . ?" encourage them to explain further and show that you're interested in understanding them better.

Avoid interrupting. It's tempting to jump in with your own thoughts or advice but try to hold back. Let them finish their thoughts completely before you respond. This gives them the space to express themselves fully and shows respect for their perspective.

Be empathetic. Try to put yourself in their shoes and understand how they're feeling. Say things like "I can see why you'd feel that way" or "That sounds really tough." Empathy helps build a stronger connection because it shows you're not just hearing their words but also feeling their emotions.

Respond thoughtfully. After they've finished speaking, take a moment to think about what they've said before responding. This helps you give a more thoughtful and meaningful reply, rather than just reacting quickly.

After you've spent time talking, take a moment to restate back to them what you heard them say. Maybe even summarize what you heard them say. Think about their feelings, their views, and what you've learned about them. How did this feel? How did the other person respond to you when you did this? Did you notice anything positive?

Active listening is a skill that can strengthen your relationships and make you a better friend. It shows that you value and respect the other person, and it helps you understand each other better. So next time you're in a conversation, try to listen actively and see how it changes the way you connect with others. By practicing love in this simple but profound way, you can build deeper, more meaningful connections with those around you.

Let's look at some illustrations to drive the idea home.

Illustration 1: The Overwhelmed Classmate

Maya noticed that her classmate Becky seemed overwhelmed lately. So, she decided to invite her to hang out at the local park. Instead of discussing her own stresses or giving advice, Maya simply asked, "Is everything okay?" That's when Becky opened up about her struggle to manage schoolwork, soccer practice, and social life.

While Becky described her situation, Maya had to make an effort not to interrupt with her own stories or suggestions. It was hard, and even though Maya thought she had some helpful advice to offer, she kept her thoughts to herself and just listened. As she did, Maya observed the worry in Becky's eyes and noticed how she played with her bracelet when talking about her upcoming projects.

After their talk, Maya realized the extent of Becky's challenges, trying to handle so many things at once. The next time Maya noticed Becky having a hard time, she was able to lend a sympathetic ear, and offer support, like sharing her notes or suggesting they study together, because she now had a deeper understanding of the stress Becky was under.

Illustration 2: The New Kid in Town

James had recently moved to a new town and was the unfamiliar face in school. During lunch, instead of joining his usual friends, Mark decided to sit next to James. He struck up a conversation, asking James about his previous town, what he missed most, and how he felt as the new student in this school. Mark noticed the emotions in James's voice, the homesickness was evident when he talked about his old friends (his tone of voice became softer), and a hint of unease (looking away or at his feet) when discussing his efforts to fit in here.

From their conversation, Mark didn't just learn about the places James had been but he got a good sense of James' previous experiences. Mark then introduced James to some of his friends with similar interests, aiming to make James's adjustment to the new environment a bit smoother.

Illustration 3: The Quiet Teammate

During a practice session, there was one teammate, Rina, who always seemed irritable and easily frustrated. Many of the other players avoided her because of this. One day after practice, Jake, curious about what might be behind her attitude, decided to sit next to her and genuinely ask about her weekend plans. To his surprise, Rina opened up, revealing that she had been caring for her ailing mother, which had been taking a toll on her emotionally and physically, leading to her irritability. She also shared some memories of hiking during her less stressful times, and how it always gave her a sense of peace. She wished for that time again.

Jake listened attentively, sympathizing with Rina's struggles, and admiring her strength. From their chat, Jake not only learned about her situation but also recognized how caring she was, how hard she was working, and her need to find temporary escapes. The next week, when the team was brainstorming activities for team bonding, Jake proposed a hiking trip, thinking Rina might like it, and that it could be a chance for the team to support and understand her better.

IN ALL THREE illustrations above, which emphasize active listening, young people were showing their love by really listening to others so they could understand how those others feel and act. This helped them get a good idea of what it's like to walk in someone else's shoes. It might seem simple, but active listening is a big part of forming strong friendships that are based on getting each other and showing one another respect—both important aspects of love.

Final Thoughts about the Lover

In this chapter, we explored the incredible power of the Lover, the part of you that seeks joy, connection, and genuine experiences. The Lover is all about rediscovering the wonder you felt as a child, seeing the beauty in everyday moments, and forming meaningful relationships based on authenticity and love. This part of you will remind you to savor each moment and appreciate the interconnectedness of all things.

Love is one of the most powerful forces within you. It's not just about romantic relationships; it's about the connections you form with yourself, others, and the world. Love gives you the strength to face challenges, the courage to be vulnerable, and the joy of shared experiences. It fuels your creativity, resilience, and ability to see the good in every situation. The Lover also reminds you that you are deserving of love just as you are, and you can expect this unconditional love to be a source of immense strength and fulfillment.

Your brain is wired to support the Lover within you. The connections you make and the habits you form are shaping pathways in your brain that will last far into the future. Practicing the skills of love, empathy, and genuine connection strengthens these pathways and will make it easier to draw upon the Lover in the years to come. The process of building and reinforcing your new neural connections is crucial, as it will build a strong base for your emotional and social well-being.

Your brain will be continually adapting and growing based on your experiences and the practices in which you engage. By consciously choosing to embrace love, kindness, and connection, you will be training your brain to support these positive behaviors and attitudes. The more you practice love and connection now, the more naturally they will come to you in the future.

As we conclude this chapter, remember that the Lover is always within you, ready to help you embrace life with open arms and build a supportive network of trusted relationships.

Do your best to remember that love is not just a feeling but also an action: a demonstration of kindness, empathy, and genuine connection. By embodying the Lover in an active manner, you will bring more love into the lives of the people around you, creating a ripple effect of positivity and fulfillment that will feel gratifying to you.

Your heart was designed to feel love and your brain was designed to think like the Lover. Embrace the learning and experiences ahead, knowing that each moment of practicing love strengthens the neural pathways that power the Lover within you.

CHAPTER FIVE

....

THE HEALER

C hildren exhibit a natural inclination to help and heal. This isn't just about tending to cuts and scrapes but also about caring for the emotional well-being of others. You might remember times when you shared your toys or comforted a friend in distress by talking with them and bringing them a favorite food or a comforting object. There is an innate kindness you possess that makes the world a better place for everyone else.

Even in infancy, children display empathy for other living things—people, animals, plants, fish, bugs, and even inanimate objects. For example, when one baby hears another crying, the baby might start to cry too, echoing the other's show of feelings. This is not learned behavior but an inherent part of being human. As toddlers get older, they begin to show care in more explicit ways, such as offering a toy or a hug to a friend in tears.

Often children express their caregiving abilities through play as well, pretending to be doctors and nurses caring for their toys and pets. These are examples of kids enacting the behaviors they have seen modeled by adults soothing siblings or animals, and are part of a genuine desire to provide comfort and assistance.

As we grow older, our innate desire to help others becomes more focused and intentional. This can be seen when teens come up with new ideas for how to face challenges impacting others. For example, kids in an elementary school might organize a recycling program to help protect the environment or start a kindness club to make sure everyone in their school feels included and supported. Middle school students often lead initiatives like collecting food for a local food bank, creating a school garden to promote healthy eating, and starting a campaign to reduce the use of plastic in the community. Each of these actions is part of longer-term efforts to create positive change and build a better future for everyone.

The Healer

In this chapter, we will delve into another dimension of who you are as a person. The Healer is the part of your personality that's bent on caring for and supporting others, as well as yourself. While this dimension of you shares qualities with the Lover (which emphasizes deep connection and profound appreciation), the Healer is mainly interested in alleviating pain and suffering. It is distinct in its focus on healing those who are sick, injured, or hurt in some way, including troubles of the heart and mind.

When you tap into the Healer within you, you can provide support to others who are upset or injured by empathizing with their pain and creating a nurturing environment for them that's conducive to recovery. For instance, you might comfort a friend going through a tough time by listening and offering kind words, volunteer at an animal shelter to help injured animals, or start a peer support group at school to help you and your classmates deal with your stress and anxiety. The Healer's intuitive insight allows it to identify the root causes of issues, and its empathetic connection brings joy and fulfillment when helping others overcome hardships.

A well-developed Healer will hone our listening and communication skills to create a safe, nonjudgmental space for open expression. This aspect in us can provide guidance and resources for healing, rooted in a belief in transformation and personal development. Importantly, the accomplished Healer part of us will be careful not to undermine the independence or confidence of others to heal themselves. Acting as the Healer, you will learn to interact with others in ways that demonstrate confidence in their own strengths and abilities to pick themselves up and move forward.

In adulthood, the Healer plays a vital role across various domains, including healthcare, therapy, counseling, coaching, and spiritual practices, embodying the ability to foster wholeness through empathy, compassion, and proactive support. I loved accessing the Healer in myself so much that ultimately I made psychotherapy my profession. You may find a profession of your own where your Healer can shine too, but you don't have to be a professional healer to express healing traits. That's a decision that can wait.

Awakening the Healer

As a teenager, you might help a friend who is struggling with anxiety by listening to them without judgment and encouraging them to use coping strategies they've learned. You don't need to have all the answers, and you should not insist that your friend follow your advice. In fact, don't give any advice. Just listen and ask questions. As the Healer, you are there—with their permission—to help them discover the healing resources they have within themselves and can access in the community around them.

If you are a talented listener, you could volunteer to be a peer mentor at school, offering guidance and support while reinforcing your classmates' abilities to solve problems and make decisions on their own. These types of actions demonstrate the Healer's role in empowering others to harness their own strengths for healing and growth.

Your own life's challenges, while often painful, may provide valuable lessons that help you understand and empathize with others. Innately, we are wired to turn our setbacks into opportunities and spin gold from straw, so to speak. Our problems, pain, and suffering aren't for nothing because they can be transformed into lessons that will aid someone else's recovery and relief. Have you heard the adage "What doesn't break us, makes us stronger"? Well, it's true. Our solutions to our problems can be shortcuts for other people to cope with their version of the same problems. This understanding is crucial for offering meaningful help and support.

There is an almost magical quality to being able to help ourselves by helping others. Many adults, including doctors, lawyers, teachers, and counselors, can tell you how often they benefit from the time, effort, and resources they devote to someone else's healing and recovery. A doctor who has experienced an illness may become more compassionate and understanding toward her patients afterward. A lawyer who has faced personal hardships may become more empathetic and dedicated to helping his clients overcome their legal struggles. A teacher who struggled as a child with learning difficulties may be able to offer more effective support to students facing similar challenges.

When you experience physical or emotional pain, you will gain insight into what others feel that you might not have had otherwise. For example, a scraped knee can help you empathize with a friend's injury. Emotional experiences, like feeling left out during a group activity, struggling with a tough subject in school, or dealing with a family tragedy, can enhance your ability to support friends facing similar struggles. Your own challenges will teach you what helps and what doesn't.

If listening to music or talking to a friend helped you through your tough time, you might suggest these activities to a friend in need. You won't always get it right, you might not say or do the right thing, and others may not always be ready to receive help, but that's okay. Sharing your experiences sends the message that you are there when they are ready. Your willingness to connect and be a supporter can make a significant difference, even if you can't always see how.

Healing Community

How do certain people become people who express their inner Healer? It's because it doesn't seem right to them to keep all they've learned from overcoming challenges in their own lives to themselves. Plus, they lighten their own load by sharing their experiences and compassion, while spreading hope—hope that the world isn't as indifferent, mean, or crazy as we may fear it to be.

Sometimes being the Healer just means offering a smile and "hello" to someone. Sometimes it means opening a Warhammer store.

Once, when I was attending a conference and we were all on a break for lunch, I stopped in a Warhammer store. If you aren't familiar, that's okay. I sure wasn't. *Warhammer* is a tabletop wargame set in the far future (year 40,000). There is a detailed universe for players to explore through gameplay that is populated by armies of miniature dwarves, goblins, and orcs. I was drawn to the window of this store on my walk, and took the opportunity to stop in. I had been wanting to learn about the game and the books related to it that seem to fascinate so many young people these days.

My impulse was rewarded. In fact, the first person I met was the owner of the store, Lucas. He and his wife were there, along with their absolutely gorgeous eighteen-month-old girl who was busily wobbling around picking items up, then putting them down again. Lucas was an Iraq veteran. Shortly after returning home from serving in the war, he had discovered *Warhammer*. In his words, "The game saved my life." Outside of his store, he also runs groups teaching young people how to play the game and how to paint the figurines that go with it.

The day I came in, there happened to be a group of five twenty-to thirty-year-old men sitting and painting and talking at one of the tables. "See these guys?" Lucas whispered. "They would never have met if it weren't for this. Each one is so different, coming from such a different background. And that's one of the things I love about this game. It brings people together, no matter where they are from."

The guys, with their fine-haired paintbrushes, little marine figurines in their large hands, sat and joked, swapped stories, and laughed. They didn't seem to be at a loss for conversation, that was for sure. It probably helped that they had something to do with their hands while they hung out. Still, they weren't even talking about the game and what they were painting. They were talking about their lives. It seemed like a group of old friends who hadn't seen one another in a while. I sure would have liked to spend the rest of the afternoon with them instead of going back to the stale professional conference I was stuck at.

As I left the store, having bought two books that Lucas recommended as primers on the subject of *Warhammer,* I also felt like I had just met someone I never would've met otherwise. Which was part of the point of this little store, as Lucas said.

Mission accomplished, Lucas. Well done.

What drew me into that store? Well, for one, I wanted to learn more about what my clients are interested in so I could connect with them better. Understanding the specifics of their interests would give us more things to talk about and additional ways for us to relate to each other. Secondly, I was curious about how knowledge of a futuristic game involving mega-marines, chaotic demons, and a warring civilization in space could become useful to their healing and growth. I'm a fan of the "whatever works" school of psychology—in case that wasn't clear before. If exploring their favorite game could help my adolescent clients open up, feel understood, or find new ways to cope in life, then it was worth learning about.

The world can be enough of a discouraging place. If we aren't careful, discouraging images become all that we see, which is tragic. Fortunately, there are people like Lucas all around us, giving to others and embodying the kindness the world needs now. These people who have access to their inner Healers remind us that we aren't alone, that someone sees us, cares about us, and understands what we are going through—often because they've been through something similar. Because they know how hard life can be, these supportive people are willing to step in and help shoulder the burden we carry.

I used to be intimidated by people I didn't know and worry they would scoff at my ignorance or view me with contempt. But then I learned to activate my Healer. The Healer in you helps you to see the human being across from you. It reminds you that they are just like you, even if they are a different age, color, gender, or background. We are the same. We are people living in a world that isn't always comfortable and often is hard. Our world is filled at times with uncertainty, pain, loss, and hope. And each of us is just trying to do the best we can with what we have got. Which is all anyone can ask of us.

When you stop to simply recognize and sit with your shared humanity with other people, it becomes almost impossible not to find common ground and build a connection with them. This connection can be a lifeline for healing. In the end, connecting with others is one of the surest and best ways to make the world a bit less scary for you and them.

Through Adversity Comes Understanding

Being a teenager involves many challenges, and learning how to overcome these experiences will help you grow and understand life better. Each difficulty you face equips you with knowledge and empathy, enabling you to be a better friend when someone needs advice, a listening ear, or simply someone who understands them.

As you get older, your resilience will expand due to having had a broader range of experiences. For instance, you may get experienced at managing academic pressure or balancing your school-work with extracurricular activities. Navigating social dynamics will also enhance your resilience by teaching you to handle your emotions constructively. Given time, you will become more adept at finding solutions to interpersonal challenges.

Every time you overcome a difficult situation, you'll gain valuable insights that can possibly help others. Sharing the details of your difficult experiences allows others to let their guard down, as they see parts of themselves in your story of strife. This helps them not feel patronized or condescended to, and instead fosters a sense of mutual understanding and support. In the bigger picture, this ability to connect through shared experiences binds us together as a society.

Seven Simple Acts That Will Give Your Social Life a Boost

You may have noticed how small acts of kindness, like holding a door open for someone or offering someone your seat, can brighten someone's day. If you haven't done so purposefully yet, try it. Kind gestures can create a chain of positive actions, from inspiring others to do the same in turn.

Performing kind acts has biological mechanisms that support them. When you engage in altruistic behavior, your brain releases important chemicals like dopamine, serotonin, and oxytocin. Dopamine, often called the "feel-good" or "reward" hormone, enhances your mood and provides you with a sense of pleasure. Serotonin helps regulate your moods and reduces your perception of stress, promoting a feeling of well-being. Oxytocin, known as the "love" hormone, fosters your sense of connection and bonding with others. Studies have shown that these three neurochemicals improve mood and overall mental health, demonstrating that kindness and altruism have tangible benefits for both you and others in your community.

Some common, yet powerful gestures of kindness and healing that you could practice engaging in are:

- Helping a Classmate. Aiding a friend with homework provides academic and emotional support.
- Including Others in Your Activities. Inviting a new student to join you promotes belonging and emotional well-being.
- Being a Good Listener. Listening to a friend's worries or woes offers them a safe space for expression.
- Complimenting Your Peers. Genuine compliments uplift people and improve their self-esteem.
- Supporting Extracurricular Activities. Cheering on friends shows care and encouragement.
- Standing Up Against Bullying. Defending others contributes to a safer environment.
- Sharing Positive Messages on Social Media. Posting positive messages fosters community and collective healing.

Create Space for Kindness

Life today is so busy, so hectic. Still, even with a busy schedule, there's time for kindness. Small gestures like the ones described above can make a significant impact and start a ripple effect of positivity that's like dropping a stone into a body of water.

Imagine a high school student named Alex who notices that a new student, Jordan, seems to be struggling to fit in and often sits alone at lunch. Alex decides to invite Jordan to join his lunch group. This small act of kindness makes Jordan feel welcomed and less isolated.

After joining the lunch group, Jordan, feeling more confident and accepted, starts participating more frequently in class and also joins a club where he makes more new friends. Inspired by Alex's kindness to him, Jordan also starts to reach out to other students who seem lonely or excluded. He invites another new student, Taylor, to join his club.

Taylor, who has been feeling overwhelmed and homesick, finds comfort in his new friendship with Jordan. He decides to start a peer support group for students like him who are dealing with similar feelings of homesickness and anxiety. This peer group becomes a safe space where students can share their experiences and support each other.

The support group grows and starts collaborating with the school counselor to organize mental health awareness events for the entire student body. These events educate the broader school community about mental health and promote a culture of empathy and support.

The initial small act of Alex inviting Jordan to lunch has now led to a series of positive changes that have impacted everyone. As a result, the overall atmosphere at the school becomes more inclusive and supportive. Students are more likely to look out for each other and offer help when needed. But the benefits spread further. Outside of school, some students from the support group begin volunteering at local shelters and community centers, inspired by the support they received and feeling eager to make a contribution. Their actions inspire others in the community to get involved, creating a wider ripple effect of kindness and healing.

See how a single act of kindness can expand into a whole series of positive actions? Crazy, right? Crazy, and cool.

The Neglector

Baptized in pain, raised in indifference, and praised for cruelty, the Neglector is a Dark Legion member that thrives on despair. The Neglector is out to sabotage your healing abilities. It is a master of imposing self-criticism and neglect, discouraging self-care, and diminishing sensitivity to others' needs. This leads to painful isolation and insecurity.

For example, when you fail a test, the Neglector might do its level best to make you feel like you were not smart enough and to discourage you from asking for help or studying harder in the future. If you have a fight with a friend, the Neglector can convince you that you're unworthy of friendship, making you withdraw and feel even more lonely. When you're feeling down, the Neglector might persuade you to skip activities you usually enjoy, telling you it's not worth the effort, which only deepens your feelings of isolation.

Surprising absolutely no one, neglecting others is also a tactic of the Neglector. If a friend reaches out to you for support, the Neglector might convince you that you're too overwhelmed with your own problems to be helpful, causing you to ignore their needs and damaging the friendship. And if a family member asks for a favor, the Neglector can make you feel like you don't have the energy or time, leading to feelings of guilt and strained relationships.

The Neglector is the voice in your head that makes you ask, "What have others done for me?" or "Why should I help them?" It makes you doubt that they will appreciate your efforts and even fear they might take advantage of your kindness. By focusing solely on your own despair, the Neglector keeps you from connecting with and supporting those around you, furthering your sense of isolation and insecurity.

Primary thinking traps of the Neglector include ideas like:

- "Others wouldn't help me, so why should I help them?"
- "If I help someone, I will be consumed by their problems."
- "The world is a just place—and people get what they deserve."
- "The pain and suffering of others is not my problem."
- "People are weak and deserve my contempt."

Nine Tactics of the Neglector and Their Impact

The Neglector's tactics all revolve around creating imbalance—whether it's making you neglect your own needs or pushing you to ignore others. The unifying theme? The Neglector's goal is to undermine healthy, balanced care, leading to strained relationships and emotional depletion. Here are nine ways the Neglector affects you adversely.

Tactic 1: Guilt about self-care. The Neglector convinces you that taking time for yourself is selfish and you should feel bad whenever you prioritize your own needs. By making you feel that others' needs are more important, you neglect your own well-being. The impact? This leads to burnout and emotional exhaustion, ultimately diminishing your ability to support others effectively.

Tactic 2. Promoting neglect of others' needs. At other times, the Neglector may push you to ignore the needs of those around you, suggesting that your efforts are wasted and unappreciated. *The impact?* Tactic 2 strains your relationships, because, as you become disconnected and indifferent, it fosters resentment and misunderstanding.

Tactic 3. Creating a cycle of self-criticism. The Neglector magnifies your every mistake and shortcoming in your mind, leading to constant self-criticism and doubt. *The impact?* This tactic undermines your confidence, making you less effective and more likely to withdraw from helping others.

Tactic 4. Fostering insecurity and fear. The Neglector amplifies any belief you may have that you are not capable of making a positive difference. *The impact?* This results in you feeling more helpless and hopeless, behaving more distantly and aloof, and avoiding meaningful connections and interactions.

Tactic 5. Undermining the importance of balanced care. The Neglector blinds you to the importance of maintaining a balance between caring for yourself and others, promoting extreme behaviors of either self-neglect or neglect of others. *The impact?*

This leads to dysfunctional relationships and a lack of mutual support, weakening the overall ability of the community to heal and thrive.

Tactic 6: Overreliance on others. Encourages excessive reliance on someone else for emotional support, to the detriment of your own well-being. *The impact?* You lose your sense of identity and worth, leading to burnout and resentment.

Tactic 7. Poorly defined personal boundaries. Blurs personal boundaries, pushing you to overextend yourself emotionally and physically. *The impact?* This leads to feelings of being overwhelmed, exhausted, and potentially exploited.

Tactic 8. Stepping in uninvited. Urges you to offer support without being asked, intruding on personal journeys and hindering personal growth. *The impact?* This tactic creates dependency and prevents others from developing their own coping strategies.

Tactic 9. Trying to control uncontrollable situations. Fosters a desire to control aspects of situations or people's lives beyond your influence. *The impact?* Tactic 9 leads to frustration and stress when things don't change, harming your mental health.

AS YOU CAN SEE, the Neglector's tactics all throw you off balance, pushing you to neglect your own needs or overextend yourself for others. By understanding how they work, you can recognize its influence in your life and take steps to counteract its negative effects.

Negative and Limiting Core Beliefs Promoted by the Neglector

Core beliefs are deep-seated views we hold about ourselves, others, and the world. These beliefs shape how we see and interact with everything around us. They can be positive and empowering or negative and limiting. Often, these core beliefs operate below the surface, influencing our thoughts, feelings, and behaviors without us even realizing it.

It may seem that as people grow older, they become less concerned about the welfare of others, as their own goals, ambitions, and needs take center stage. And yes, this can happen, although not as much as you might think from watching the news or social media videos of outrageous behaviors from entitled or demanding individuals exhibiting selfish or inconsiderate behavior, or even people in positions of authority, like the police, who are supposed to be helping the general public stay safe. Yet, the desire to help and understand others is deep within us from the start and remains as we grow older. But why do some of us stop showing this care and empathy as adults?

As we grow, many factors can influence and change our core beliefs and our ways of relating to others. The Neglector takes advantage of these influences to instill harmful beliefs that hinder kindness and empathy, such as the following ones.

Societal pressures. The Neglector uses societal messages that praise looking out for "number one" and discourage showing "weak" emotions, making us forget the importance of being kind and caring. Because of this, we suppress our empathy and avoid showing care for fear of being perceived as vulnerable, leading to a belief that showing kindness makes us weak.

Negative experiences. The Neglector exploits our bad experiences, such as being let down or hurt by others, in order to convince us that being kind or open will only lead to more pain. To protect ourselves, we then become detached, building walls around our emotions and forming the core belief that connecting with others only leads to hurt and disappointment.

Busy and stressful lives. The Neglector capitalizes on our hectic, stress-filled lives, making us prioritize material gains over kindness. As a result, we begin to value people on the basis of what they can do for us rather than who they are, fostering a belief that people are tools for achieving success rather than individuals deserving of kindness and connection.

These negative experiences, social pressures, and a harried lifestyle can all warp our perception of ourselves, others, and the world, ultimately forming harmful core beliefs that limit our ability to connect and care. For example, if you believe you are not likable or you annoy others, this core belief may dictate how you act toward people. You might expect people to be cold and rejecting, leading you to act distant and aloof to protect yourself from getting hurt. Because you are so focused on expecting rejection, you might not notice when others are actually friendly or interested in getting to know you. Over time, this belief forms a self-reinforcing cycle where your expectations and actions continually confirm your negative view, even if it's not true.

Worthless Will

Let's look at a specific example of a self-fulfilling prophecy. Imagine a student named Will who has a core belief that he is worthless and no one loves him. This belief leads to many automatic thoughts that seem to prove him right. For instance, if a friend doesn't invite Will to hang out one weekend, Will immediately thinks, *See, my friend doesn't really care about me. He just feels sorry for me and thinks I'm pathetic.* And if a teacher doesn't call on Will in class, he thinks, *I must not be smart enough to be noticed.*

Even when people are kind to him, Will tends to dismiss it, thinking, They're just being nice to look good and impress others. They don't really like me.

Core beliefs are the ideas we have about ourselves and our worth deep down inside. These beliefs shape how we think about and react to all kinds of situations. If you believe *Nobody loves me,* this idea can influence your thoughts in many ways.

Take a closer look at the thoughts Will struggles with each day. These negative core beliefs can lead to self-fulfilling behaviors that seem to confirm their validity, even when opportunities exist to find out differently.

Example: *My mom and dad never listen to what I have to say.*

- Reality: Will's parents are often busy, but they do listen when they have time. Will focuses on the times they are too busy.
- Self-fulfilling Behavior: Will might stop sharing his thoughts and feelings, which would strengthen his belief that his parents never listen to him.

Example: *Dad never has any time for me.*
- Reality: Will's dad works late during the week but makes time for family activities on weekends. Will overlooks these positive moments.
- Self-fulfilling Behavior: Will might withdraw or refuse to participate in family activities, making it seem like his dad really doesn't have time for him.

Example: *My brother always gets what he wants, but I don't.*
- Reality: Will's brother got to go out with friends, but Will recently went to a concert he wanted. Will only remembers his brother's outing.
- Self-fulfilling Behavior: Will might not appreciate or ask for things he wants, reinforcing the belief that his brother always gets what he wants while he doesn't.

Example: *Everyone else but me gets to choose what to watch on television.*
- Reality: The family takes turns choosing shows, but Will only remembers when it wasn't his turn.

- Self-fulfilling Behavior: Will might not participate in choosing shows anymore, reinforcing the belief that he never gets to choose.

Example: *If we fight, I always get the blame.*
- Reality: In arguments, Will feels targeted, but sometimes he also gets an apology from his sibling or parent.
- Self-fulfilling Behavior: Will might become defensive or aggressive in arguments, making it more likely that he will be blamed, reinforcing his belief.

Example: *Mom doesn't think my jokes are funny.*
- Reality: Will's mom sometimes doesn't laugh at his jokes, but often she does. Will fixates on the times she doesn't laugh.
- Self-fulfilling Behavior: Will might stop telling jokes or engaging with his mom humorously, reinforcing the belief that she doesn't find him funny.

Example: *My friends never include me in their plans.*
- Reality: Will feels left out when he hears about plans he wasn't invited to, ignoring times he was included.
- Self-fulfilling Behavior: Will might isolate himself or stop reaching out to friends, reinforcing the belief that he is not included.

Example: *Teachers never notice my hard work.*

- Reality: Will focuses on the times a teacher didn't praise his effort and forgets the times the same or another teacher did acknowledge his achievements.
- Self-fulfilling Behavior: Will might stop putting in effort or participating in class, reinforcing the belief that teachers don't notice his hard work.

The Neglector always tries to persuade Will to see things in a darker, more negative light, pushing him away from relationships and relegating his inner Healer, his own ability to help and heal others, to the sidelines. This negative influence keeps Will trapped in a cycle of self-fulfilling behaviors that reinforce his negative core beliefs. Meanwhile, Will continues to suffer and bury himself in behaviors that make it harder and harder to see the truth.

By recognizing these patterns and challenging his negative core beliefs, Will can create opportunities to see things differently. For instance, by choosing to share his thoughts with his parents even when they seem busy, or by participating in family activities, he might find that his beliefs are not as accurate as they seem. Engaging positively with his family and friends can help him realize that he is valued and included, breaking the cycle of negativity.

This shift can help break the cycle of self-fulfilling behaviors and lead to more positive interactions and self-perceptions. As Will starts to see the truth, he can reconnect with those around him, offer support, and begin to change for the better. By overcoming the Neglector's influence, Will can cultivate healthier relationships and a more positive outlook on life.

Healer Training

Developing the Healer and defending against the Neglector requires consistent effort. The exercises in this training section are simple in design. Even so, they can be hard to put into practice consistently. As you do, I believe you will find them rewarding enough to encourage you to keep working on them. Each exercise is intended to build on the previous one, ensuring that you start building a more solid foundation of empathy, self-compassion, and resilience before moving on to the more complex and challenging practices.

These exercises focus on basic skills such as identifying and nurturing empathy, challenging your negative thoughts, and fostering self-care habits by setting personal boundaries.

Exercise 1: Identifying and Strengthening Your Inner Healer

Start an empathy journal. This can be as simple as having a notebook you carry in your backpack or keep in a dresser drawer where you make notes of your natural compassionate actions. The idea is to notice and reflect on these important times so your awareness of your behavior grows.

Instructions. Each day, write down instances where you felt empathy for someone or acted compassionately. Reflect on how these actions made you feel and how they might have impacted the other person.

Sample entry. "Today, I helped a classmate with their homework. It felt good to see them understand the material, and they seemed grateful. It also helped me understand the lesson in a new way as well, which makes me feel more confident in the class."

Expectations. Through this practice, you will become more aware of your empathetic actions, boosting your confidence and reinforcing your natural inclination to help others.

Indicators of success. You may:

- Notice an increased frequency of empathetic actions.
- Receive positive feedback from those you help.
- Experience a greater sense of fulfillment and purpose.

Once you're accustomed to journaling about your empathy, begin to log acts of kindness in your empathy journal. Regularly practicing kindness will help embed empathy and compassion in your daily routine, making these qualities a natural part of who you are.

Instructions: Create a log in your journal with a small act of kindness for each day. These acts can be simple, like giving a compliment, helping someone with a task, or listening to a friend's concerns. Track your progress and reflect on these acts made you feel and how it seemed to affect others.

Expectations. By logging your acts of kindness, you will develop a habit of kindness, leading to more positive interactions and stronger relationships.

Indicators of success. You find that:

- You consistently complete daily acts of kindness.

- Your relationships noticeably improve.
- You feel happier and more connected to others.

Exercise 2: Create and Practice Positive Affirmations

Positive affirmations can help reframe your thinking about self-care, reminding you that it is a necessary and positive practice, not something to feel guilty about because you might feel it is selfish or a waste of time. In this exercise, you will first invent the affirmations you want to instill in your mind and then you will repeat them.

Instructions. Write down positive affirmations that reinforce the importance of self-care. For example: "Taking care of myself allows me to help others better" and "I deserve to be happy and healthy."

Read these affirmations daily, especially if you feel guilty about self-care, and speak them aloud while looking at your reflection in a mirror. If you want to take this to the next level, sing them to the tune of your favorite song.

Expectations. You will begin to view self-care as essential and positive, helping to reduce feelings of guilt.

Indicators of success. You enjoy:

- Reduced feelings of guilt when practicing self-care.
- Engaging in self-care activities more frequently.
- Improvements in your overall well-being and energy.

Exercise 3: Practice Thought Checking

By questioning and reframing negative thoughts on the spot, right when they occur to you, you can disrupt a cycle of self-criticism and develop a healthier, more balanced mindset.

Instructions. When you notice a negative thought, pause and write it down. First, ask yourself:

1. "Is this thought helpful?
2. "Is it true?"
3. "What evidence do I have for and against it?"

Then, replace the negative thought with a more balanced, positive one. For example, you could replace the derogatory thought "I'm selfish for wanting time alone" with the better thought "Needing time alone to recharge so I can be more present for others, isn't selfish."

Expectations. You will become more skilled at recognizing and countering negative thoughts, leading to increased self-esteem and emotional resilience.

Indicators of success. You discover:

- The frequency of your negative thoughts decreases.
- Your self-talk becomes more balanced and positive.
- Your mood and self-confidence improve.

Exercise 4: Establish Boundaries and Balance

Healthy boundaries prevent burnout and promote mutual respect in relationships, which is crucial for sustainable caregiving. Boundaries are the emotional and psychological guardrails that keep you from being overwhelmed, mistreated, or taken advantage of by clearly defining what behaviors you will and won't accept from others. They help you protect your time, energy, and emotions—like saying no to extra work when you're already overloaded, refusing to engage in toxic conversations, or insisting on personal space when you need it. Follow the steps below to strengthen your boundaries and enhance your well-being.

Instructions. There are six steps to strengthening boundaries.

- Step 1: Identify Weak Boundaries. Reflect on areas in your life where you feel drained, taken advantage of, or find it hard to say no. Pinpoint situations where you overextend yourself or where your boundaries feel unclear or disrespected.

- Step 2: Clarify Your Needs. Determine what boundaries would help protect your time, energy, and well-being. Consider what's important to you and what limits need to be set to support these priorities.

- Step 3: Develop Clear Boundaries. Create specific boundaries for different areas of your life (for example, work, family, friendships). Be as concrete as possible about what you will and won't accept, and why these boundaries matter.

- Step 4: Communicate Your Boundaries. Share your boundaries clearly and respectfully with others. Use "I" statements to express your needs (for example, "I need some uninterrupted time to focus on my work").

- Step 5: Practice Saying No. Learn to say no in a firm but polite manner when a request or expectation goes against your boundaries. Remember, saying no is about prioritizing your well-being, not rejecting others.

- Step 6: Evaluate and Adjust. Regularly reflect on how your boundaries are impacting your relationships and personal health. Adjust as needed to ensure they continue to support your well-being and healthy connections.

By following these steps, you can develop and maintain boundaries that protect your energy and enhance your relationships.

Expected Outcome. You will feel more in control of your time and energy, leading to healthier relationships and better self-care.

Indicators of Success. You find that:

- You feel more comfortable saying "no" without guilt.
- Your relationships become stronger and more respectful.
- Your personal well-being improves, and you experience less burnout.

BY INCORPORATING THESE exercises into your daily routine, you can strengthen the Healer and defend against the Neglector. Developing self-awareness, challenging negative beliefs, practicing self-compassion, and engaging in positive actions will help you break a cycle of negativity and foster a more balanced and fulfilling life.

As your Healer grows stronger, you'll find it easier to connect with others and offer your healing presence, creating a positive environment for everyone around you.

Final Thoughts about the Healer

The world will always need healing as it goes through difficulties and changes. Today, young people like you are being bombarded every day with negative messages about existential threats such as climate change, nations at war, and death and suffering caused by disease and poverty. These types of messages leave many of us, but especially young people, feeling demoralized and helpless, and retreating into a mindset focused on scarcity, self-protection, and the fear of disaster around every corner. This negativity is made more virulent by the Dark Legion and bad actors like the Neglector, which are our natural instincts for healing and self-preservation twisted and turned against us and others.

The good news is that you can untwist these instincts in yourself. It's an action worth doing because the world so badly needs your healing presence in it. You do not need to make grand sacrifices or launch gigantic initiatives to play a role in world healing. You can start at home, right in your own backyard so to speak, with the people and places you visit each day. Throughout history, the Healers within us have driven humanity's progress in the fields of science, medicine, and community support. Our relentless pursuit of health and recovery reflects humankind's deep-seated need to ensure our survival and well-being. And today, by harnessing the power of the Healer, we can continue—

collectively and as individuals—to make remarkable strides in improving the quality of life for ourselves and those around us.

As you move forward, remember that healing is a journey which requires ongoing effort and dedication. By nurturing your inner Healer and protecting against the Neglector's negative influence in your mind, you can create a more caring and supportive world for yourself and future generations.

CHAPTER SIX

THE SEEKER

No one is exactly what they seem. This might sound pretty cynical, but it's true in a lot of ways. As you get older, you'll start to notice how differently you and others act in various situations. At first, this difference might be confusing or even a little unsettling. But it's really no stranger than the difference between how you would behave in church instead of at a party. All of us have many facets to our personalities.

Have you ever heard a story from a friend of your parents or your grandparents about that loved one, maybe from the time before you were born, and in hearing this story discovered something completely new about your parent or grandparent even though you thought you knew them well? What about you? If you were to ask them, would people say that they really know who you are? This could be a tough question for them to answer, especially when you're still figuring things out for yourself.

Do you know others as they understand themselves, deep down, or as the people around them see them, from outside? It is possible, if not likely, that you could list all the people in your life and find that very few know everything there is to know about you. They might know that you play a sport or have a hobby, but not how you feel from day to day. Do they know you when you're super excited and happy, or only when you're feeling stressed, nervous, disappointed, or defeated?

There's a saying: "Your earthly name is what others call you, but your true name is known only to God." Whether or not you believe in God, it is true that you are more than just an accumulation of experiences, conditioning, and socialization. You are more than just a series of electrical and chemical reactions in your brain. Just as you have a name given to you in our physical world, you also have a deeper essence that may be called by another name, perhaps one you can discover for yourself.

In this chapter, we will explore the Seeker. The Seeker is the Champion that goes beyond surface-level labels, activities, moods, and expectations. The Seeker is there to help you to understand yourself and your purpose. It's the part of you that craves a complete, intimate, all-around view of your abilities, strengths, weaknesses, passions, and values. It is the aspect of you that desires a full understanding of how you fit into the larger picture of your community, the world, and even the universe, and what this means for your life story. This part of you spends time wondering what your purpose is and what difference you make in the grand scheme of things.

You are developing an identity right now. The term *identity* refers to the qualities, beliefs, personality traits, and ways of expressing yourself that make up who you are as an individual. Your identity will evolve as you mature, develop new skills and interests, and go through different life events. It encompasses all your values, experiences, and how you see yourself in relation to the world. Who you think you are today will change over time.

Sometimes people don't discover important things about themselves—or know how to articulate them—until they are forty or fifty years old (sometimes even older). This isn't a bad thing. It's natural because life is a continual process of discovery and self-understanding.

Your identity is influenced by various factors, including family, cultural background, friendships, peer groups, and where you go to school. As a teen, these influences play a crucial role in shaping who you are and how you see yourself.

Family is often the first and most significant influence on your identity. The values, traditions, and beliefs you grow up with can have a profound impact on your sense of self. For instance, if your family places a high value on education, you might develop a strong academic identity and prioritize learning. Your ethnicity and cultural background also will shape your identity, as it provides a framework of customs, languages, and practices from dance styles to favorite foods—that influence your worldview and sense of belonging. You may be a champion dancer of salsa, polka, or hip-hop. You may eat pasta, pad thai, or hamburgers every night.

Friendships and peer groups are equally important as family during adolescence. The people you choose to surround yourself with can influence your interests, behaviors, and self-perception. Positive friendships are those which provide you with support, validation, and a sense of belonging. For example, if you have friends who are passionate about sports, you might be encouraged to join a team and develop an athletic identity. Whereas negative peer influences are those which lead you to engage in risky behaviors and self-doubt.

Where you go to school also plays a role in shaping your personal identity. Schools offer students various opportunities for self-discovery through extracurricular activities, academic programs, and social interaction. Joining clubs, participating in sports, or engaging in community service projects can help you explore different aspects of your personality and interests. Additionally, the environment and culture inside a school building can impact your self-esteem and sense of belonging. A supportive and inclusive school culture can boost your self-esteem, encourage personal growth, and provide a sense of belonging, while a negative environment may hinder self-expression and contribute to feelings of isolation or inadequacy. Where you spend your days and who you spend them with has a lasting influence on your confidence and overall sense of self.

As a teen, you typically will express and explore your identity in various ways. These can be either positive or negative. On the positive side, after volunteering at a local shelter, you might realize that you really enjoy helping others. This realization then could lead you to pursue a career in social work or healthcare. Or after joining the school newspaper, you might discover a passion for writing, which could influence your decision to major in journalism or creative writing in college. The more kinds of experiences you have, the more you can find out what you like and don't like to do. This information will shape your identity and guide your future choices.

Realistically, identity exploration can have negative aspects. Some teens experiment with drugs or alcohol as a way to fit in with their peers or to rebel against perceived constraints. Others struggle with peer pressure or adopt negative self-perceptions due to bullying by their classmates or harmful, mean-spirited comments. Such experiences can lead to self-doubt and negative self-beliefs.

In college and adulthood, the process of personal discovery continues. Imagine someone who has worked in finance for twenty years and feels unfulfilled for most of that period. At forty-five, they take up painting or photography as a hobby and realize it brings them immense joy and satisfaction. Not only that, but they discover they have a real talent or a good eye for assessing the talent of others. This newfound passion might lead them to transition into a career as an artist or open a gallery. Another example could be a person who, after years of working in corporations, decides to travel the world in their fifties and discovers a love for teaching English abroad. These experiences can significantly alter their sense of self and life direction. A forty-two-year-old divorced mom might decide to express her entrepreneurial spirit and start a business once her kids are old enough to cook their own dinner.

The more you realize what is important to you, what you value at any given phase of your life, and who you admire and respect, the more you will begin to behave in ways that reflect these insights. Maybe it's standing up for a friend who's being treated unfairly because you value loyalty, choosing not to join in on gossip because you believe in kindness, or pursuing your passion for music or sports even if it's not considered "cool" by others. As you navigate different experiences—both positive and negative— you'll naturally learn more about your true, authentic self.

Identity development is an ongoing journey. The beliefs you develop about yourself through experiences as well as from what other people tell you to be true will significantly shape your identity. Understanding these connections to how you feel and think about yourself can help you navigate the complexities of self-identity. When others tell you that you are capable, kind, or intelligent, it reinforces positive beliefs about yourself. When you encounter challenges and overcome them, these experiences can solidify a resilient and empowered self-view. Compare that to how you would feel if someone told you, "You'll never amount to anything in life because you're a schmuck."

The great thing is that you can take matters into your own hands and choose which remarks to believe and which to ignore entirely. And you can deliberately do things to improve your level of confidence. Or even make yourself feel better on a day when you feel upset about making a mistake or disappointed because you got a lower grade than you wanted on a quiz.

To develop a strong, positive identity, it's important to critically evaluate the messages you receive from others and your interpretations of your experiences. Recognize that you have the power to reshape these beliefs and align with who you want to be. Embrace the journey of discovering who you are, knowing that it will continue to unfold throughout your life.

Beyond Labels and Limits:
Take Charge of Your Story

People say that everyone has a different image of us than we have of ourselves, and a different image than anyone else has of us. So basically, we're like those abstract paintings—everyone's looking at the same thing, but nobody agrees on what it is! If this is true, then each person you meet will have a different impression of who you are and you will mean something different to each of them. You are not just one thing, and you're not stuck in one version of yourself. You do have a choice in the matter.

The reality is that different parts of you show up depending on who you're with, what you feel like expressing, where you are, and what challenges you're facing. Bringing these parts of yourself together into a whole picture, where you understand your many strengths, limits, hopes, fears, and regrets, is something you'll work on throughout your life. Sometimes you will be more intentional about how you bring these parts of yourself into alignment, but often this will happen on its own. Gradually.

If you're lucky, you'll keep being surprised as people reflect parts of you to you that you weren't fully aware of having or had ignored. This is one reason why we seek out other people. Sure, it's for their company, reassurance, support, and some laughs, but it's also because of how we explore and define different parts of ourselves. We play roles, act out parts, and try out different ways of being, thinking, and feeling to see what fits best, what aligns with our deepest beliefs, and who we want to be. The real power is in your ability to choose which direction you want to take and which parts you build upon and refine.

We all grow up in different types of families, whether it's with a traditional mom and dad, splitting time between two divorced parents, living with a single parent, or being raised by a same-sex couple. Maybe you grew up in a multigenerational household, a blended family, or experienced life in the foster care system. Families come in many forms. No matter the situation, as we interact with family members, we begin to shape our sense of self by how they see us. But what they see and tell us isn't necessarily who we truly are.

You are part of a complex world full of invisible systems that shape how you live your life. For instance, every family has its own patterns of behavior, rituals, routines, and habits that make them unique yet similar. The details may be different, but the story is the same.

Consider a family where every Sunday evening is dedicated to a family dinner. This ritual strengthens family bonds and it also instills our lives with a sense of routine and togetherness. Another example might be a family that values education, encouraging reading and doing homework every night. This routine helps develop discipline and a love for learning.

In some families, the pattern might include celebrating cultural or religious holidays with specific traditions, like lighting candles during Hanukkah or preparing special meals during Ramadan. These rituals connect family members to their heritage and provide a sense of identity and belonging.

The whole world is full of repeating patterns. In nature, we can see these patterns everywhere: in the shapes of trees and lightning bolts, the arrangement of leaves on a stem, the symmetry of butterfly wings and flower petals, and the spirals of galaxies, hurricanes, and snail shells. Animals follow patterns too, like birds flying south for the winter or whales traveling to warmer waters. Just as nature and animals follow these repeating patterns, the routines and rituals in your family shape your daily life and contribute to your identity.

Cultural norms shape how people behave in different societies, influencing everything from how we greet one another to the clothes we wear. Similarly, habits are routine actions we perform without much conscious thought, like brushing our teeth or taking the same route to school every day. Both norms and habits create a sense of order and predictability, which helps us navigate daily life.

Life, however, is filled with various other patterns beyond cultural norms and habits. Psychological patterns reflect common ways of thinking and feeling, such as fearing the unknown or yearning for a sense of belonging. Life cycle events like being born, graduating, getting married, and dying—are also significant patterns that mark transitions in our lives. These events are often accompanied by shared rituals or traditions that give them added meaning. Although some occur only once or twice in a lifetime, they leave a deep impression on us because of their emotional impact. Living in a shared culture means that people often experience and interpret these events in similar ways, adding to a collective understanding of what it means to be human.

The point is: you are part of this intricate web of life. Even more importantly, you have the power to shape how these patterns in your life unfold. You can break free from restrictive rules or routines, influence how people see and experience the world, and contribute to positive change. Whether through deliberate action or spontaneous adventure, your choices have the potential to inspire others to explore beyond their limitations, making life richer and more fulfilling for everyone.

Your personality is a combination of how you think, feel, and act. It develops from a mix of your genetics, environment, and experiences and continues to change and grow throughout your life. By understanding your personality, you can learn more about how you interact with the world and respond to different situations. Recognizing these patterns in your personality can help you understand your strengths and areas for growth.

Mistakes Are Opportunities for Self-Discovery

Whenever people deliberately try to define who they are, they set themselves in motion and inevitably will make wrong turns. If you haven't made one yet, you will. This is okay, and to be expected. It is part of the learning process. A lot of times the wrong turns lead to rocky relationships, meaningless sex, drugs, and any number of other pleasures (food, games, thrill seeking) without conscience. While such things might give us temporary satisfaction, they ultimately lead to profound feelings of emptiness and disconnection.

Relying on external validation or sensory pleasure for happiness or relief from emotional pain can distract us from the pursuit of a deeper understanding of ourselves and may even create a cycle of dependency and dissatisfaction. This means that when you constantly seek approval from others or look to temporary pleasures to feel good, you get out of touch with your true self and what genuinely makes you happy. This behavior leads to a never-ending loop where you need more and more external approval or pleasures to feel satisfied, because what you're chasing can never truly fulfill you. In this case, you would be dependent on the same things that could never give you what you need.

In addition, you can also take a wrong turn if you completely reject all the joys and pleasures of the world. After noticing all the risks involved in reaching for what you want, you might decide that it's better to start living a narrower, more deprived life. This means turning away from natural desires and pleasures. You might choose this way of life to prove your desires can't control you, or that you are more than just a bunch of sordid instincts or animalistic urges. But while discipline and self-control are important, an extremely self-denying lifestyle is also going to lead you to isolation and disconnection.

The world is filled with pleasures that allow us to experience the richness of being alive. Despite this, many stories and beliefs warn against indulgence. For example, the story of Adam and Eve portrays the consumption of the apple, following the advice of a snake, as a symbol of the hidden dangers in our desires. Similarly, myths suggest that masturbation leads to blindness, or that enjoying good food results in gluttony and moral decay.

Psychologically, pleasure is essential for a balanced and fulfilling life. It enables us to connect deeply with ourselves and others, and to truly appreciate the beauty and wonder the world has to offer. When embraced mindfully and in moderation, pleasure enriches our lives and fosters our well-being. After all, why would anyone want to get out of bed in the morning if life were only about work and pain? Pleasure motivates and sustains us, making the journey of life more meaningful and enjoyable.

A world of drudgery and disappointment is exactly what many young people see today. They watch adults die from heart disease, cancer, alcoholism, and strokes, which science says may be linked to stress. To them, adults appear to be working themselves to death. Some parents seem to be on an endless treadmill of work with little time to enjoy their families and the fruits of their labors. They own large houses yet live at the office, driving expensive cars to their 60–70-hour workweek jobs. It's no surprise young people seeing this wonder what the heck they have to look forward to in their lives. They ask, "What? You're telling me I have to work hard to get into a good college, then work hard in college to get a good job, then work hard and sacrifice at my good job to have a good home, then work hard to keep that job pay for all the good things, and on and on? No thanks. I'm good. You go ahead. I'm going to just chill right here on the couch."

The lie in our culture is that money, fame, and material things will make a person feel whole and complete. That you will finally achieve "nirvana" when you just have enough money— "so, sign up now to get our weekly newsletter to tell you how to live your best life for only $19.95 a month."

How does this make any sense? Instead, what you and other young people today see are people getting sick and dying prematurely, getting divorced, becoming strangers to their families, and suffering mental illnesses at record highs. If you see all this and wonder, *Is that all there is?* you're not alone.

You aren't crazy if you have questions about how things seem to be done today. It's the Seeker within you raising these questions. It knows you won't find true fulfillment on the path of consumerism. *Consumerism* is the belief that personal happiness and success are achieved through the acquisition of material goods. Proponents of consumerism measure people's worth by how much they own and constantly seek more possessions as a way to find satisfaction.

Instead, the Seeker within you seeks balance, recognizing that both fun and discipline are important in life. Each makes the other seem more rewarding and has a place in defining our lives. Happiness true satisfaction come from mixing these parts, realizing that your worth isn't based on how much fun you have or how much you avoid it.

Finding yourself means exploring different desires and aversions, understanding what drives you or never could, and finding a way to live that respects both your dreams and your natural human feelings. This approach helps you enjoy life while also staying focused, leading to a more satisfying and balanced existence. By embracing this balance, you can navigate life's challenges and pleasures in a way that fosters genuine contentment and growth.

The Seeker knows there is a bigger picture and that every experience, whether fun or serious, helps you grow. This is the journey that helps you find your true self, discover who you want to be, and realize you can have an important purpose in life.

Identity Construction Begins on Day One

Since you were born, your brain has been automatically learning how to think, feel, and act. It's like a fish that just swims without ever needing lessons and doesn't even notice the water it's in. One of the first ways this starts is through the sex you are born as, which begins a cascade of messages and experiences that shape how you view yourself. From the moment you are identified as male or female, societal expectations and norms begin to influence your self-concept.

For instance, boys might be encouraged to be tough, competitive, and emotionally reserved, while girls might be guided toward being nurturing, cooperative, and expressive. These early messages come from parents, teachers, media, and peers, all reinforcing certain behaviors and discouraging others based on gender expectations.

As you grow, these learned behaviors and thoughts become so familiar that they can seem like an inseparable part of you, just like your physical traits. This is called *conditioning*. Conditioning makes it very hard to see where the things you automatically do out of habit end and you begin.

Your brain tries to make a complex world more coherent by simplifying it for you. This simplifying is very useful, and primarily it helps you survive. However, it also simplifies how you think about yourself. You become a boiled-down abstract idea of yourself, instead of what you really are, which is much more complex. Your brain will also fall into what is called a *fixed mindset*, which is where you believe that who you are is unchangeable. For example, you might see yourself as socially awkward because of a few awkward experiences you have had or judge your worth by the grades you got during one school year. Simplifying your identity in this manner may cause you to overlook other, socially graceful experiences and other, better grades.

You're not alone in being influenced by this tendency to simplify. We all tend to categorize people based on assumptions, often putting both ourselves and others into small boxes. Stereotypes are mental shortcuts designed to help us make quick decisions, but they limit how well and accurately we perceive the world. For instance, you might believe that boys are naturally better at math and girls are more nurturing. This belief, however, is a stereotype about gender that has been passed down through generations. When we internalize such stereotypes, they shape how we see our own abilities and those of others, impacting our behavior and expectations. As long as these stereotypes persist, they restrict everyone in our society and prevent us from recognizing our true potential.

The great thing is, as you grow up, you can start thinking differently just because you want to or your common sense proves an idea is mistaken. You don't have to stay stuck with social conditioning. You can learn and change. When you do test your assumptions, you'll begin to see different sides of yourself and of others. You will also learn that the ideas you had were only a small part of the bigger picture.

By understanding how social expectations based on gender are shaping your self-concept, you can start to question these influences and develop a more nuanced and true sense of self. Challenging your own beliefs is a process that may help you appreciate the complexity and diverse possibilities for who you can become, beyond the constraints of your early conditioning.

This process is like peeling an onion. Each layer you remove reveals more depth and complexity, both in yourself and in others. For example, if you're a boy who loves cooking, you might initially feel pressured to pursue sports instead because of societal expectations. However, after questioning this norm, you can begin to embrace your passion for cooking and see it as a valuable part of who you are. Onions always remind me of cooking, so I just had to use it as an example.

Similarly, a girl who enjoys building things and working with tools might feel out of place in a male-dominated field such as engineering or mechanics. But by challenging gender-based expectations, she can confidently pursue her interests.

As you grow and change, you will naturally become more aware of the layers of abilities and interests you possess and start seeing the deeper essence of people, including yourself. You will come to understand that everyone has a rich, multifaceted personality that extends far beyond the initial stereotypes you might attach to them. This broader understanding will enrich your relationships and your perspective on life.

For instance, you might have a friend who is incredibly good at sports and also loves to write poetry. By acknowledging and appreciating these two aspects of their identity, you will see them as a more complete person. And save room to learn even more facets of their personality than these! Right now, learning to recognize your own diverse interests and talents will allow you to break free from limiting labels and embrace a fuller version of yourself as you enter adulthood with all the roles and responsibilities that are involved.

Ultimately, peeling back any disguises to reveal additional layers of who you are to friends and family helps you build more authentic connections with them and enhances your understanding of your identity. Taking the risk to share who you are, for real, encourages you to build a life for yourself that is true to who you are, rather than one that merely conforms to restrictive social norms simply to play it safe and be accepted. Having deep self-awareness is the key to a fulfilling and enriched life.

College is a great time to engage in this kind of growth and self-discovery largely because it gives you much more freedom and new responsibilities. Because it takes you outside the home you grew up in and possibly to a new geographic location far away, you will meet people in college who don't have preset ideas about you, and you will be able to form relationships with the people you meet on new terms. This is why so many young people find life after high school to be so liberating. You get to redefine who you are and let go of old labels and expectations that kept you tied down. It's like outgrowing the toys you once played with or the clothes you wore before you had your last spurt of new height.

The truth is, the Seeker in you knows you are not just a passive receiver of your surroundings but an active participant in shaping them. You have the power to change and influence what's happening in your immediate environment. You are in control of your life to at least some degree—and would be in control of even more of your circumstances if you attempted to do so purposefully.

You might find that the pressure to excel and conform to narrow definitions of success is overwhelming. This pressure, not surprisingly, often leads to anxiety, depression, and burnout. However, once you understand that you have the power to shape your environment and determine some of the events taking place in your life, you will be able to start prioritizing activities that keep you from falling into these traps. By listening to the Seeker part of yourself, which knows more than you are consciously aware, you can gain more insight into what truly inspires you—the pursuits that truly resonate with who you are and offer the greatest satisfaction. By tapping into the Seeker's wisdom, you can start to make your activities and goals match your passions.

The Seeker can help you in your journey to self-understanding and fulfillment. It does so with a particular style of thinking, that includes:

- Curiosity. The Seeker is always wondering "what if" and trying new things just to see what happens.

- Interest in Learning. Every day is a school day for the Seeker, not just in classes, but in life. The Seeker is constantly picking up new skills.

- Mulling Things Over. The Seeker takes the time to reflect on experiences and interactions to learn from them and grow.

- Being Cool with Change. The Seeker embraces change as an opportunity for growth and improvement.

- Keeping Open Ears and an Open Mind. The Seeker aims to listen to others respectfully, without judgment, considering different perspectives before forming an opinion, making a decision, or disagreeing.

- Taking Chances. The Seeker courageously explores new opportunities.

- Authentic Communication. Engaging in meaningful conversations is one of the ways the Seeker is able to deepen your connections with other people.

- Living Your Truth. The Seeker helps you make choices aligned with your values and beliefs, even if these differ from the values and beliefs of others.

Adopting a Seeker mindset means each day becomes an opportunity to explore, grow, and connect with others. Even the smallest experiences become chances to learn and push your personal boundaries, making life more interesting and, for many, exciting.

The Deceiver

Psychologically speaking, the Deceiver is the Seeker's main rival, using illusions to twist reality and lead you away from knowing your true self. The Deceiver is like a modern-day Loki, the mischievous god from Norse mythology. Just as Loki uses deceit to sow confusion and chaos for his brother Thor, the Deceiver distorts your ideas about yourself and, in doing so, causes chaos for you. By planting seeds of doubt and manipulating your perceptions, the Deceiver tries to convince you that you are something you're not, hiding your essence and potential.

Imagine walking into a funhouse at an amusement park, where you encounter a hall of mirrors. These mirrors create funny and confusing distortions of how you look, sometimes leading you into a disorienting tailspin. The Deceiver part of your cognitive activity is like those warped funhouse mirrors, constantly putting images and ideas into your head that make you see yourself in a distorted way. For instance, you might look into one of these mirrors and see yourself as extremely tall and thin or short and wide, completely different from your actual appearance. While this can be amusing in a funhouse, it can be harmful when it comes to your self-perception.

The Deceiver whispers lies and half-truths about how you should act and who you must be, creating fear about stepping beyond the boundaries erected by the world around you. It's the voice in your head that says, *You have to look a certain way to be accepted* or *You must follow this path to be a good person.* This voice convinces you that there is enormous danger in stepping outside these imposed boundaries, making you fear any deviation, because it is sure to lead to disaster.

Let's take a look at some examples of how this happens in a few situations.

Your career choices. You might love art and nonetheless end up choosing a career in finance because the Deceiver convinces you that an artistic career isn't practical. Believing being an artist will lead to financial instability, you suppress your true interests and follow a safer, more conventional path, feeling unfulfilled and disconnected from your true self.

Social situations. In a group of friends who value certain behaviors or interests, you might pretend to enjoy things you don't really like or hide parts of yourself that you think won't be accepted. The Deceiver tells you that being authentic will lead to rejection, so you put on a facade, which ultimately makes you feel isolated and misunderstood.

Your personal relationships. You might stay in an unhealthy relationship because the Deceiver convinces you that being alone is worse than being with someone who doesn't treat you well. The fear of loneliness or social judgment keeps you trapped in a situation where you can't be your true self.

The Deceiver highjacks your brain's simplifying mechanisms to create overpowering beliefs like:

- "I am what others say I am."
- "I am what I do. My worth comes from my achievements and actions."

- "I am my body. My physical appearance defines me."
- "My identity is tied to my relationships. I need to be accepted by everyone, or else I'm a loser."
- "If I want to keep my friends, I must think like them. If I don't follow the group, I'll be left out."

Negative Impacts of Deceptive Beliefs

Let's explore how these deceptive beliefs can negatively impact our behavior. Below are some examples I've encountered repeatedly in my practice. Each scenario is a blend of multiple cases to ensure privacy and confidentiality are maintained.

If You Are What Others Say You Are

If this is your belief, then your self-esteem and mood will fluctuate based on what you think others believe about you, making you dependent on external validation. If you don't get it, you will experience painful emotional swings.

Example: Emily, a sophomore, struggled with math and often found herself frustrated by difficult problems. In middle school, her teacher once said, "Some people just aren't math people," which stuck with her. At home, her older brother jokingly called her "Miss Calculator" whenever she asked for help, implying she couldn't do the work on her own. Even her best friend casually remarked, "It's okay, you're more of a creative type." The Deceiver used these moments to convince Emily that math was simply beyond her, and when she faced another setback on a tough assignment, she was ready to give up, believing her failure was proof she wasn't smart enough.

Analysis: The Deceiver made Emily internalize these offhand remarks, interpreting them as confirmation of her inability, rather than seeing her struggles as part of the learning process. This belief undermined her confidence, making her feel inadequate in math.

If You Are Your Body

If this is your belief, then you will fixate on how you look on the outside and neglect how you feel on the inside. This thinking can lead to unhealthy behaviors that could develop into more serious issues, like eating disorders.

Example—Sue: Throughout high school, Sue often heard comments from family members like, "Are you sure you need a second helping?" or "You'd look so much better if you just lost a little weight." Friends would casually remark, "You're pretty, but you'd be stunning if you slimmed down a bit." These comments made Sue hyperaware of her body. She started skipping meals, thinking it was the only way to be considered attractive. On social media, where everyone seemed flawless, Sue felt like she didn't measure up, further feeding her belief that her value was tied to her appearance.

Example—Kevin: In middle school, Kevin was teased by other boys who called him "string bean" or "toothpick," and said things like, "No one is going to be interested in a shrimp like you" and "Real men don't have scrawny arms." Even his coach once said, "Hit the weights, kid, or you're never going to be able to compete."

Over time, Kevin started feeling like the stereotypical ninety-pound weakling who gets sand kicked in his face at the beach. He became obsessed with bulking up, spending hours in the gym and overloading on food, desperate to escape the "shrimp" label. He believed that if he didn't get bigger, he would never be seen as masculine or desirable.

Analysis: The Deceiver convinced both Sue and Kevin that their value was tied to how others perceived their bodies. Sue internalized the comments about her weight, which fueled her belief that she had to be thinner to be worthy of attention or affection. Kevin's insecurity about his size, compounded by the feeling of being the weakling everyone mocked, led him to believe he had to transform his body to fit a masculine ideal. Both became trapped in a fixation on external appearance, neglecting their mental and emotional well-being, and developing unhealthy patterns of behavior in the process.

If You Are Who You Love and Want to Be With

If you believe this, you may feel incomplete without the approval or presence of others. You'll rely on romantic relationships to validate your self-worth, often sacrificing your own needs and interests to maintain the relationship.

Example: John, a teen in a new relationship, was deeply in love with his partner, who had very different interests and goals. His partner loved art and theater, while John was passionate about sports and music. Subtle comments like, "You'd enjoy this more if you gave up on those games," or "We don't really fit in with your crowd," slowly chipped away at John's confidence. The Deceiver convinced him that to keep his partner happy, he had to give up his own passions and adopt theirs. John began to doubt that his interests had any value.

Analysis: The Deceiver led John to believe that his self-worth was tied to his partner's approval, making him feel that he needed to conform to keep the relationship. This undermined his sense of self, convincing him that he wasn't good enough on his own to deserve love.

If You Must Think Exactly Like Your Friends

If you believe this, you'll feel pressured to adopt the beliefs and behaviors of those in your social circle, even when they don't match your own. You'll suppress your individuality to avoid conflict or rejection, prioritizing conformity over authenticity.

Example: Alex enjoyed spending time with his friends, but they had very strong opinions on fashion and trends that clashed with his own. The Deceiver convinced Alex that to stay accepted by the group, he had to adopt their style and viewpoints, even though they didn't align with his personal tastes. Alex felt that if he expressed his true preferences, he would be ostracized.

Analysis: The Deceiver made Alex believe that to belong, he had to conform to his friends' beliefs and tastes, erasing his individuality. This pressure to fit in led him to suppress his real self, putting him at risk of losing self-respect and authenticity.

If Your Worth Comes from Your Achievements and Actions

If this is your belief, you'll feel immense pressure to succeed academically, athletically, or socially. Any failure or setback may cause your fragile sense of self to crumble, leaving you feeling worthless.

Example: Anita, a high-achieving student and athlete, always prided herself on excelling in school and sports. However, when she failed to make the varsity soccer team, the Deceiver immediately took advantage of her disappointment. "You're not good enough," it whispered, "Without this, what do you have to show for yourself?" Anita began to question her value, convinced that without her success in soccer, she was a failure in all areas of life.

Analysis: The Deceiver made Anita believe that her entire self-worth was tied to her achievements, leading her to see a single setback as a reflection of her overall inadequacy. Instead of recognizing failure as a normal part of growth, Anita felt that her lack of success defined her, causing her confidence to unravel.

Seeker Training

The Seeker within you can see through illusions and help you focus on what you want. The Seeker knows that your real fulfillment can only come from embracing your passions, facing your challenges with determination, and staying true to yourself, not from folding under the pressure of those around you or believing in the lies that the Deceiver tells you. The Seeker knows that you will always feel better when you stand on your own two feet and don't abandon your values or dreams out of fear.

Exercise 1: Your Personal Interests

The objective of this exercise is to help you gain clarity about your personal passions and interests, evaluate the pros and cons of pursuing them, and overcome any limiting beliefs that may prevent you from following what excites you. By the end of this exercise, you will create a practical action plan to pursue your passions while addressing any realistic concerns.

This exercise is divided into four steps.

Step 1. Explore your passions. Write down activities and subjects that genuinely excite you. Think about hobbies, classes, or projects that you engage in (or did at some point in the past) which make you lose track of time because you enjoy them so much. For example, you might write down: "I love painting and drawing. I can spend hours creating art without getting bored."

Step 2. Make a pro and con list. Make a list of pros and cons for pursuing your passion versus following a safer, more conventional path.

For example: Pursuing art as a career.

- Pros of Pursuing Art: Fulfillment, creative expression, potential for unique career opportunities.
- Cons of Pursuing Art: Uncertainty, potential financial instability.

For example: Choosing finance as a career path.

- Pros of Choosing Finance: Stability, clear career path.
- Cons of Choosing Finance: Lack of passion, feeling unfulfilled.

Step 3. Challenge the Deceiver's lies. Identify the Deceiver's lies about pursuing your passions, then counter them with the truth. For example:

- Lie: "An artistic career is impractical and will lead to financial instability."
- Truth: "Many artists have successful and financially stable careers. I can combine my passion with practical steps to ensure stability."

Step 4. Make an action plan. Think about a plan to pursue your passion while addressing practical concerns. Try to include actions in your plan, like learning what you would need to learn, how you could practice, and people and places you could go to with your interests.

Example: If you decide to major in graphic design in college, you could plan to take business courses to learn about managing your finances and begin, with the support of your college professors and other mentors, to build a portfolio to showcase your best work.

Exercise 2: Your Social Situations

The objective of this exercise is to help you feel more comfortable and confident being your authentic self in social situations, even when your interests differ from those of your peers. By following the five steps, you will practice expressing your true self, reflect on your social interactions, and challenge any limiting beliefs that may prevent you from being genuine. Ultimately, you will develop small, actionable goals to improve your sense of authenticity in social settings.

Step 1. Identify real interests: Write down activities you genuinely enjoy, even if they are different from those of your friends.

Example: "I love reading fantasy novels and playing the piano."

Step 2. Do some role-playing. Practice being authentic in an accepting environment. Role-play with a trusted friend or family member on how to assertively express your true interests and opinions in social situations.

Example: You could practice mentioning your interest in fantasy novels. Then find opportunities to casually drop bits of information into conversations about stories you've read and the characters in them. Use only tiny bits of information to check the listener's level of interest. Even though if your friends usually talk about sports, you may find that the more you talk about the books you like, the easier it gets.

Step 3. Reflect on outcomes. After a social event, reflect on instances when you were authentic versus when you put on a front. Write down how each made you feel. For example, you might write: "When I talked about fantasy novels, I felt nervous at first, but then relieved and happy when my friend seemed interested. Playing along, pretending to like sports, felt exhausting and made me feel fake. Like they would find out I really wasn't interested, and then not like me."

Step 4. Challenge the Deceiver's lies. Identify the lies the Deceiver tells you about being authentic and counter them with positive truths. For example:

- Lie: "Being real will lead to rejection."
- Truth: "My true friends will accept me as I am, and being myself will help me find those people. There is nothing wrong with having different interests."

Step 5. Set small authenticity goals. Set small, achievable goals to be more authentic in social settings.

Example: Share one genuine interest with your friends each week. Perhaps telling them about a movie you watched over the weekend and liked.

Exercise 3: Rid Yourself of Unhealthy Relationships

The objective of this exercise is to recognize unhealthy relationships and prioritize your well-being. There are four steps.

Step 1. Identify what you want in a relationship. Write down the qualities that are important to you in a relationship and why. For example: "Honesty, mutual respect, and emotional support are really important to me. Especially since I have had times when people have not been totally honest, and I want to avoid this happening in the future."

Step 2. Assess your relationships one by one. Think about some of your relationships, to see how they match up to what you want. Write down instances where your needs are not being met. For example, you might write: "My close friend often dismisses my feelings and doesn't support my interests. This makes me feel like there is something wrong with me, and that I can't be open with him/her."

Step 3. Challenge the dating and friendship relationship lies. Identify the lies the Deceiver tells you about staying in unhealthy relationships and counter them with positive truths. For example:

- Lie: "Being alone is worse than being with someone who doesn't treat you well."
- Truth: "I deserve to be in a relationship where I am respected and supported. Everyone needs time alone. In fact, time by myself can help me focus on myself and what I really want."

Step 4. Create a safety plan. When ending an unhealthy relationship, it's important to plan carefully, especially if you're concerned about your safety. This plan could include seeking support from trusted friends, family members, a counselor, or, in cases of violence or threats, involving the police.

Example: Amara had been feeling increasingly uncomfortable in her relationship and decided it was time to break up. She was worried her partner might react angrily or become threatening, so she talked to her best friend and the school counselor for support. Together, they helped her sort through her fears and figure out how to communicate her decision safely.

Amara decided to meet her boyfriend in a busy, public place to talk, which would reduce the chance of things escalating. She made sure her friend knew when and where the conversation would take place and checked in afterward to confirm she was okay. Having this support system and safety plan helped Amara feel more confident and secure as she ended the relationship.

Exercise 4: Countering Harmful Ideas about Who You Are

Navigating adolescence and the transition to adulthood can be challenging, no doubt. Especially with the constant pressure about what to do and not to do from peers, society, and the media. It's easy for your sense of self-worth and identity to become distorted by ideas that lead to feelings of inadequacy and confusion. As previously mentioned, the Deceiver, a chief instigator of misleading thoughts, can make you believe that your worth is tied to others' opinions of you, your achievements, your appearance, and your relationships.

As you progress through these exercises, a clearer picture of who you are will come into focus. This clearer sense of self will help you decide how you want to live. Clarity like this can act as a sort of shield against the Deceiver's most harmful messages and help you stick to being who you are and want to be in the future.

Beliefs about ourselves often stem from our life experiences, many of which can leave lasting impressions. For example, being told you're "fat" or "selfish," not being invited to a friend's party, or not making the team can deeply impact how you view yourself today.

These experiences may lead to unhelpful beliefs that hold you back. This exercise will help you explore those beliefs and begin breaking free from them.

Step 1: Identify Your harmful beliefs about who you are.
Take time to reflect on negative beliefs you may have formed from past experiences. Write down specific situations that may have contributed to these harmful ideas about yourself. Many people fall into mental traps that keep them stuck in self-doubt and insecurity. Let's look at a few real-life examples of harmful beliefs.

- Belief: "I'm not good enough because I didn't make the varsity team." *Situation*: You were really excited to try out for the team, but when you didn't make it, you felt like a failure. Now, you believe you're not as talented as others.
- Belief: "I'm fat, so I'm not attractive." *Situation*: Friends or family made comments about your weight, leading you to feel insecure about your body. Now, you think people only see you for your appearance.
- Belief: "I'm selfish because I focus on my own goals." *Situation*: A family member called you selfish when you didn't do something they wanted. Now, you question whether pursuing your own dreams is wrong.
- Belief: "I'm only valuable if I get perfect grades." *Situation*: You've always been told that success equals good grades. Now, you feel like any academic slip-up means you're not smart or worthy.

These beliefs are examples of mental traps that can limit your potential and make you feel stuck.

Step 2: Challenge the Deceiver's mental traps. For each harmful belief identified in Step 1, challenge it with rational, supportive thoughts. This helps break the hold that these false ideas have over you.

Trap 1: Believing you are what others say you are.

- Counter Thought: "I am not defined by what others think. My worth comes from within."
- Evidence: "There have been times when I've felt good about myself regardless of others' comments, like when I helped a friend or completed a challenging project."

Trap 2: Believing you are what you do.

- Counter Thought: "My achievements do not define my value. I am more than my successes or failures."
- Evidence: "Even when I don't get perfect grades, I'm still creative, kind, and thoughtful, and those traits matter."

Trap 3: Believing you are your body.

- Counter Thought: "My body does not define my worth. I'm valuable for who I am, not how I look."
- Evidence: "My friends enjoy spending time with me because of my humor and caring nature, not just my appearance."

Trap 4: Believing you are who you love and want to be with.

- Counter Thought: "I am complete on my own. My relationships add to my life, but they do not define my worth."
- Evidence: "I've felt happy and confident in moments where I was single or spending time alone."

Trap 5: Believing you must adopt others' opinions to fit in.

- Counter Thought: "I can respect others' beliefs without changing mine. It's important to stay true to myself."
- Evidence: "I've kept friendships strong even when I've shared different opinions, which made me feel more authentic and accepted."

Trap 6: Believing disagreement means insult and disrespect.

- Counter Thought: "Disagreements are natural and don't mean disrespect. I can calmly express my thoughts."
- Evidence: "I've had disagreements where we worked through things respectfully, and it brought us closer."

Step 3: Define and break free from unhelpful beliefs.
Once you've identified these traps, ask yourself if these beliefs are truly serving you. Often, they are limiting and prevent you from being your full, authentic self.

Here are five tips for breaking free.

1. Be Specific. Define the belief in simple, clear terms. For example, "I believe that I need to be perfect to be loved."

2. Identify the Source. Reflect on where this belief may have originated. Did someone say something that stuck with you? Did you experience something that made you feel this way?

3. Find the Truth. Counter your belief with facts and supportive evidence, as seen in the examples above. Remind yourself of moments when you were accepted or valued regardless of that belief.

4. Set New, Healthier Beliefs. Replace harmful beliefs with affirmations like, "I'm enough as I am," or, "My worth isn't tied to one event."

5. Take Action. Slowly start living in alignment with your new beliefs. Set small goals to remind yourself of your worth, like sharing an unpopular opinion, wearing something that makes you feel good, or taking pride in an effort, not just the outcome.

By exploring where these beliefs come from and challenging them with rational, supportive thoughts, you can take meaningful steps toward breaking free from harmful ideas and embracing a more confident, authentic version of yourself.

Final Thoughts about the Seeker

As we wrap up this discussion, let's take a moment to appreciate the power of your brain and why shaping your internal story matters. You have the power to create a personal code: a set of values and principles that will guide you in leading a fulfilling and genuine life. By consciously defining what matters most to you, you can ensure that your choices support your growth, happiness, and authenticity. This way, your life will become a reflection of who you truly are, and you will be able to navigate your challenges with a clear sense of purpose and direction.

The story you tell yourself about who you are will play a critical role in how you perceive and interact with the world. This story will be built from every bit of input and experience, from the mundane to the extraordinary. Recognizing this, it becomes clear that you are not just a passive character in the story you tell yourself but its principal author. Each day provides a new opportunity to write a chapter in the book of your life that reflects your true self.

Consider the narrative traps set for you by the Deceiver, such as moments when you might feel pressured to conform to external expectations or doubt your worth based on past failures. By identifying these traps, you can counter the lies the Deceiver tells you and instead create a narrative about yourself that is true to who you are. Begin by celebrating your strengths and acknowledging your potential to grow.

Through exercises designed to fortify the Seeker within, such as setting goals for personal growth, practicing self-compassion, and challenging limiting beliefs, you equip yourself with the tools to navigate life's complexities. These activities are stepping stones to deepen your self-understanding and increase your resilience.

As you move forward, remember the importance of being mindful about the stories you tell yourself and the beliefs you accept as true—sometimes without questioning them. Your personal narrative can become a source of empowerment for you, rather than a prison sentence forcing you to live in ways you don't want to live.

Drawing upon the strengths of the Seeker, you will continuously discover yourself at different levels. And although the Deceiver may set traps to stop you, you have the strength and wisdom to get past them. You were born with the capacity to discern the truth.

CONCLUSION

Finding your natural abilities is the beginning of your journey. Alongside this discovery, it's essential to identify and connect with people you can trust and bring along with you. Often, the strengths of the people you choose to surround yourself with will complement your strengths, enabling you to manage and overcome your weaknesses. For instance, although you might have a well-developed sense of the Warrior within you, you may struggle at times to access your inner Healer or Lover. Having people in your circle who exemplify these Champions will bolster you because they provide models that you can learn from and emulate. This will make you a more well-rounded individual and amplify your strength.

If there has been one main point to this book, it is this: You are the mastermind of your life choices and the architect of how you think, feel, and act. Many players in your life will contribute to your successes; however, some may instead create obstacles for you. In the end, you are the one who puts together all the information and resources at your disposal and decides what to do with it. You can lean on the people who are supporting you on your journey by asking them for advice or to help you shake yourself out of an inaccurate viewpoint.

Understanding Your Champions

In your life's journey, you are never alone. The Five Champions within you—each representing a unique quality and resource—will always be there in your corner, having your back no matter the time or place. These personas embody the best parts of you and can guide you through life's challenges. Understanding and developing these traits will make you more confident, resilient, and true to yourself. Let's review them quickly, one more time.

The Warrior: The Warrior is the essence of courage and strength within you. This Champion is not swayed by fleeting trends or peer pressure and stands firm when faced with opposition. The Warrior defends your personal freedom to love, create, and explore. When life demands that you alter your routines—perhaps because of needing to focus more on your studies than on socializing—the Warrior is the aspect of your character that you can rely on to back you in doing so. The Warrior will empower you to pursue the changes necessary to become the person you aspire to be, rather than the person others expect you to be.

The Wizard: The Wizard is your creative energy, innovative thinking, and imagination. This Champion sees the potential in every situation, provides solutions, and discovers options. Whether it's excelling in a challenging subject or initiating a new club at school, the Wizard will guide you to attain tangible outcomes. The Wizard will teach you how to couple your creativity with knowledge to propel your personal growth and realize your dreams.

The Lover: The Lover is what leads you to form deep connections and appreciate the beauty in life and others. This Champion motivates you to pursue passions that enrich your spirit and foster genuine happiness, such as participating in environmental conservation or community service. By aiding you in discerning which paths will bring you fulfillment, the Lover will guide you to invest your energy in what truly matters.

The Healer: The Healer is the natural ability of your body and mind to regenerate and heal. This Champion recognizes the importance of self-care and of extending compassion to others, too. It views your resilience and the well-being of your community as connected. By nurturing the Healer, you will contribute positively to the world while also safeguarding your own health and happiness.

The Seeker: The Seeker is constantly on a quest for knowledge and understanding. This Champion encourages you to dive deep, ask critical questions, and explore the different possibilities that may ultimately define your place in the world. The Seeker can help you navigate information overload and societal expectations and aid you in carving out a personal identity that's aligned with your true interests and strengths. By continually seeking knowledge and understanding, the Seeker will help you uncover your true potential and find meaningful ways to contribute to the world around you.

Understanding your five Champions can help you figure out which qualities you possess that you want to develop further. It also provides direction in terms of selecting pursuits that might be interesting, rewarding, and exciting for you. A combination of Champions may play primary roles in your personal profile, and these may rotate based on specific events that you are experiencing and your objectives at any given time.

By actively taking steps to increase your self-awareness and to understand your character traits and thinking styles, you are taking responsibility for your personal power. You are embracing a critical element required for reaching full maturity: taking control of the direction of your life. This means being aware of mistakes that occurred in the past and taking steps to prevent repeating them, whether they are your own mistakes or those of others, such as your parents and friends.

A second part of developing maturity entails actively figuring out what you are good at, what you like, and with whom you get along. By doing so, you contribute to making the world a place of learning, acceptance, and love. Taking a proactive approach to making these determinations will enable you to foster deep connections, both with yourself and with others, which is a key to leading an emotionally rewarding and empowered life.

Building Your Dream Team

Finding people you are comfortable with and trust is a real game changer. This personal tribe or dream team is made up of people in your life who you trust and depend on. Worrying too much about what strangers or distant acquaintances think, especially online, only leads you off course. But having a group of people you respect and learn from is different. They're the ones who really get you and around whom you can be totally yourself.

Building Your Circles of Trust

To better understand and manage your relationships, think of them as belonging to three different circles of trust. Where you place people within one of the following three circles help you determine how much intimacy you can share with each person and how much trust you can extend to them.

Your inner circle. This is your closest and most trusted group, often including your best friend, close family members, or a mentor. These people know you inside out and support you unconditionally. They see all sides of you—the good and the bad—and provide advice that is balanced and true to who you are.

Your middle circle. These are friends and acquaintances you trust and share common interests with, but they might not know you as deeply as your inner circle. They are reliable and supportive, but you might not share your most personal thoughts and feelings with them.

Your outer circle. This includes casual acquaintances and people you interact with occasionally. They might be classmates or neighbors. While you have a friendly relationship with them, the level of trust and intimacy is limited.

Choosing the right people for each circle is important. And it's essential to recognize who belongs in your inner circle, as these individuals have the most influence on your emotional well-being. Trusting the wrong person too deeply can lead to disappointment or betrayal, while underestimating the support from someone trustworthy can leave you feeling isolated.

Your dream team might include a best friend who always has your back, a family member who understands you completely, a teacher or coach who believes in your potential, or a mentor who guides you. These people are there to cheer you on, remind you it's perfectly okay to mess up sometimes, and help you remember your worth.

Here's how members of your inner circle would support you in a real-life situation. Imagine you're struggling with a project for school. After you reach out to your dream team, your best friend, someone who's always there for you, offers to help brainstorm ideas. A teacher who believes in your potential gives you extra time and resources to complete the project. A family member listens to your concerns and offers emotional support. Together, this dream team provides a balanced support system that helps you navigate challenges and succeed.

By carefully choosing who fits into each circle of trust, you can build a strong support network that helps you navigate life's challenges and successes. This thoughtful approach to relationships ensures that you are surrounded by people who genuinely care about you and contribute positively to your life.

There are many players in your life who contribute to your successes and may create obstacles or challenges for you. In the end, you are the one who puts all of this together and decides what to do with it. Many people will help you on your journey. You can lean on them, ask for advice, or help you shake yourself out of an inaccurate viewpoint. Others are extremely important to your self-understanding and help you develop into a loving, compassionate, generous, and industrious person.

Understanding your Five Champions and the inner strengths and resources they represent will be a lifelong journey of self-discovery and personal growth that will require you to be open to change, willing to learn, and muster up the courage to pursue your passions. By taking this journey, not only will you enhance your life but you will also contribute to creating a better world for everyone you know and whose life yours touches.

The Journey of Self-Awareness Starts Inside

Like a torch, you carry the flame of your Five Champions within you. Their presence is a fundamental energy that animates who you are as a person. It is the life force behind your creativity, resilience, and potential. As you embrace this force, it will guide you through challenges, inspire your actions, and lead you to your destiny. Like all of us do, you will be lighting your own path forward.

As a young person, you need to know what you are made of and what the world "out there" is like, so that you can trust you are capable of taking care of yourself and handling things on your own. Meeting and overcoming challenges will enable you to become an adult who feels deserving of respect and is taken seriously, even admired.

The stories each of us tell ourselves, the plans we make for the future, the reflections on our past, and the difference we wish to make in the world—these all come from how we talk to ourselves. Every day for the rest of your life you will be having conversations with yourself. A lot of the time these will be versions of the same conversation, over and over. Trying to identify how the theme of your personal narrative motivates you and how to improve it is like trying to crack a big mystery. Many times, the answers you are seeking will seem to dart just out of reach right before you can grasp hold of them, like floating objects you push further away simply by grazing past them.

No matter what answers you ultimately find, one truth will always stand out from the rest: You are a valuable person and will make important contributions to the world. Big or small, your actions can impact others now and in the future. And this means that you get to decide the kind of impact you want to make. How would you like to affect the lives of others?

The narrative you write about yourself and the nature of the world will shape your reality. For if you believe there is good in the world, you will seek it out. And in doing so, I predict that you will often find good things come your way, reinforcing your belief in the world's goodness. On the other hand, if your narrative emphasizes negativity, that's what you will encounter.

Life will hold tons of inspiration for you if you are willing to recognize it. To appreciate life's broader picture, you may have to rise above the smaller annoyances, disappointments, and discomforts that are typical parts of everyday life. But if you let yourself transcend those obstacles, you'll see evidence that you are benefitting from the contributions that other people have made to the world—people who are strangers to you.

Wherever you are right now—the chair you are seated in, the light you are reading under, the vehicle you are riding in—was created by someone. And it's possible that these things were made with someone like you in mind. Although the creators might not have known it was for you at the time, here you are, enjoying their creations. In the future, other people—strangers—will benefit from your contributions similarly.

Whether you know it or not, people are drawn to you. Each of us, including you, has something unique in us that attracts certain others. It might not always be the people we want to attract, but someone is drawn to us, nonetheless. Despite any self-doubts we may have, there are others who see something in us that is worthwhile and good.

Of course, sometimes we can get so caught up in our own self-doubt that we can't see why others might like us or want to spend time with us. On these occasions, it's like we have blinders on and don't even see the person in front of us or feel the love they are giving us. At some level, nonetheless, we must recognize we deserve love, admiration, and attention. If we don't, if we shut others out of our lives, it will confirm our fear of being alone. It is a funny thing that we create the lives that matches our narratives, positive or negative.

Life is complex, and seemingly opposite things can be true at the same time. You might feel confident in one area of your life, like school or sports, for example, while simultaneously feeling completely uncertain in another area, like your social life or future career. You can love someone deeply and still feel frustrated with them. You can be excited about a new opportunity while also feeling scared about the changes it will bring. All of this is part of being human.

Contradictions are part of life. Embracing them can help you navigate the ups and downs more effectively. It's okay to feel multiple emotions at once, and understanding this can give you a more balanced perspective. Do your best to appreciate the full spectrum of your experiences because you don't have to fit into a single box or category.

Recognizing that life is full of duality—opposites and contrasts—could make you more empathetic and open-minded toward others. It may help you to imagine that others are also dealing with their own contradictions and complexity. Making room for this possibility can lead you to form deeper connections and have a greater sense of community.

Your Feelings Don't Have to Run Your Life

Your feelings are important, but they are just part of the picture. It's essential to honor and respect them because they provide valuable insights into your experiences and reactions. However, you need to manage how much influence they have over your decisions carefully.

Think of your feelings as signals. They can alert you to something that needs your attention, like feeling nervous before a big test, which might push you to study harder, or feeling joy while spending time with friends, showing that these relationships are valuable to you. Such signals are significant and deserve to be acknowledged.

But it's equally important not to let your feelings control all your actions and decisions. For example, feeling angry or hurt is valid, but acting on those emotions impulsively can lead to make regrettable decisions. Similarly, feeling afraid can protect you from danger but can also hold you back from taking positive risks or trying new things.

Balancing your feelings with rational thinking is key. If you're upset about a conflict with a friend, for example, it's important to recognize and process your upset. But when deciding how to handle the situation, consider the facts and potential outcomes alongside your feelings. Pause to consider what would be an ideal outcome and try to imagine how to work toward it. This approach will help you make more balanced and thoughtful decisions.

By weighing consequences against possible actions, you can allow your emotions to inform you without letting them dominate your ultimate choices. Often the best course of action is to find a middle ground where you respect your feelings while also using your reasoning skills to guide your actions. This balance will help you navigate life's challenges more effectively and make decisions that are in your best interest.

This point is especially important when it comes to the expression of negative emotions. If you're feeling overwhelmed by thoughts that the world is a cruel place, that no one cares for you, or that the future appears bleak, you are probably letting negative feelings do the driving. It's completely natural to believe what these feelings tell you. Emotions can easily take over our reality. But when we feel something deeply, it's very difficult to understand its meaning and what we need to do to ease it. Sometimes, you will need to give yourself some time and space to let things settle and collect your thoughts.

Any time you only see things as all good or all bad, consider that it might be because your feelings are clouding your judgment. For example, thinking life is always great and everyone's always happy might mean you're letting too much joy blur your view. This could be important if there are serious issues that need your attention. On the other hand, if you regularly see the downside in things, sadness or anger are likely controlling your thoughts.

It's not good for us when emotions make all our choices for us. For example, if you're super sad, you might decide to stop hanging out with friends or doing fun things because you're just not feeling it. But a mood can be elevated, and you can play a part in changing how you feel. Maybe watch a funny video, read an interesting story, or do something you love to take your mind off your worries. If you love animals, watch cute animal videos on Instagram or TikTok or visit a pet store. The main point is this: You do not need to be at the mercy of your feelings. You actually have choices all of the time, and that is a good thing.

Your Path to Fulfillment

When we do good things for others, we usually get goodness back in some form. Remembering to do the small things, like saying hello or smiling at someone new when greeting them, can make a big difference.

Take Jake, a guy from my high school, as an example. He was handsome, athletic, and popular. To me, it seemed like he was always surrounded by friends and constantly had weekend plans. Once, a friend managed to get us both an invite to a party at Jake's place. I was anxious about it. I didn't see myself fitting in with the "cool," popular kids because I just didn't see myself that way. So, I was expecting we'd be out of place. All this is to say, I was shocked when Jake greeted me and my friend warmly at the door, offering each of us a friendly high-five. It was clear he wanted us to feel welcome and comfortable.

And he succeeded. His friendliness felt good and immediately set me more at ease. It wasn't just Jake trying to look good to impress someone; it was clear Jake genuinely wanted everyone there for the party to feel at home. Looking back on it decades later, I can see that Jake's mastery in radiating this kind of positive energy elevated his stature in our school and explains why he was popular.

This was a very clear example to me that when you spread positivity, it not only returns to you but it amplifies and spreads further. Making the people around us feel good is one of the paths we can take to fulfillment. If your life were a loaf of bread, positivity would be the yeast—it lifts and enriches you.

Historically, humanity has always wrestled with the disruption of change and innovation. In the resulting disorder and confusion, it's natural for people to wonder where they fit in, questioning how these changes relate to their ultimate purpose, their desires, and the path to achieving them. This confusion isn't exclusive to our time. Throughout history, human societies have confronted technological and cultural revolutions. These shifts, though disruptive, follow a common pattern: cycles of upheaval, followed by periods of calm, then transformation.

In many ways, these broader societal patterns mirror the journey each of us undertakes. As children, we are curious about everything, exploring and learning as much as we can about the world and ourselves. Adolescence then thrusts us into another time of disruption and disorientation, a new phase of growth.

This cyclical nature of growth and transformation, both on a societal and personal scale, aligns with the age-old concept of the hero's journey. As portrayed in countless myths, a hero ventures from the known into the unknown, faces challenges, and eventually returns home, reborn (figuratively, as a wiser or kinder person) and enlightened.

Heroic myths are more than mere stories; they are the mechanism by which our ancestors centuries ago preserved essential lessons for future generations, helping us, their descendants, understand our experiences, learn more about ourselves, and connect with them. It is as if they are reaching through time to share their hard-won wisdom.

Novels are another way to teach lessons. I often think of Katniss Everdeen, the main protagonist in Suzanne Collins *Hunger Games* trilogy. Set in a dystopian future, these novels chronicle Katniss's harrowing experiences in the Hunger Games, a brutal annual competition where young people known as "tributes" from various districts fight to the death. Only one tribute survives each year. As the series unfolds, Katniss evolves into a symbol of rebellion against the oppressive Capitol regime. Her personal story of facing unimaginable challenges and emerging as a beacon of hope and survival mirrors the hero's journey of ancient mythology.

Heroic stories, like that of Katniss or a knight slaying a fire-breathing dragon, illustrate the profound forces at work today shaping you and your peers of the same age, including societal expectations, peer pressure, and media stereotypes. Despite the power of these forces, however, you have the choice to carve out your own destiny just like legendary and fictional heroes.

In mythology, Prometheus defied the gods to bestow the gift of fire upon humanity. In *The Adventures of Huckleberry Finn*, characters like Tom Sawyer follow their inner moral compass, often conflicting with dominant societal values, as evidenced by the pre-Civil War South setting.

In real life, heroes, such as the activist Rosa Parks, resist oppressive societal norms, too. Harriet Tubman, once enslaved herself, became a leading figure in the Underground Railroad, making nineteen trips back to the Confederate South where she risked capture and punishment, and guiding 300 enslaved people to freedom in the North. Her acts of bravery and resistance against the institution of slavery are iconic.

You are not a nameless bystander in our world. You are the hero of our own life and can stand up for what you believe in. As you face challenges or pressures that try to change you, you can stay true to your values and better intentions. The cost of neglecting your beliefs and denying what you truly think is usually much greater than the cost of honoring them, despite any blowback you might receive.

Have you ever noticed how the idea of being "average" is considered nearly as bad as failure in our culture? When we talk about a child being average, people start to get upset. For some parents, it is as if the child was called a terrible slur or has become one of the children of the damned. One parent I encountered, upon being told her child had average scores on an IQ test, hounded the clinician for weeks, demanding her child be retested and making it sound like the clinician's fault her child scored as the child did.

In a society where working at McDonald's is often seen as a symbol of wasted potential and ultimate shame, being average is treated like a modern-day leprosy to be avoided at all costs. Yet many of the youth who begin their work life behind the counter or at the griddle in a fast-food restaurant go on to receive a good education, secure interesting jobs that provide for their needs, and become respected and adored adults. And many kids who get average grades in high school have happy and productive lives as adults like me. So, you should be proud of yourself for holding a job and learning the steps of performing your role as an employee.

For some parents, however, even the information on future outcomes is still not enough to please them. The lure of perfectionism warps their idea of what qualifies as "good enough." Coping with a parent like that can be really tough. But remember, it won't be like this forever. One day, you'll be an adult and can make your own decisions without having to listen to their rules. You'll have the freedom to live life on your own terms. Hang in there!

It may be difficult to grow up in our society because this is a society that tells you that you must be a superstar, or you will have wasted your life. It sounds extreme, but this kind of message gets repeated in thousands of ways every day. Bombarded by messages in the media and in your school, you are constantly being told, "You can do anything you put your mind to."

Try to forgive your parents when they fall into such traps. They're being fed a pile of nonsense too. When educators, doctors, and politicians proclaim it is their children that will change the world for the better, they eat it up. So they might walk around thinking it will be you, their child, who cures cancer, wins an Oscar, invents teleportation, or figures out how to get six-pack abs by eating Doritos. All parents want to believe their children can be "great."

However, what society means by "great" is worth examining. Even if every child could achieve greatness, being great would simply become average, bringing you back to where you started. It's a never-ending cycle of unrealistic expectations and traps.

So, What's Wrong with Wanting to Be Great?

There isn't anything wrong with wanting to be great at something. But it's easy to confuse being "great" at something in particular with being happy and fulfilled.

Is there anything wrong with not wanting to be great? I don't think so.

The truth is, being good at something doesn't guarantee happiness. In fact, chasing greatness can sometimes get in the way of leading a happy and fulfilling life. Many people who have pursued greatness have also faced significant suffering, and when they finally reached their goal, they often found it anticlimactic. Countless individuals, after reaching the top—winning a medal or securing an award—find themselves feeling depressed and miserable, at least for a little while. Why? Because achieving their goal didn't fulfill all the high expectations they had placed on it. And because now that they reached the goal they were working toward, they need something else to live for.

Sure, there might be a short-term boost in mood and outlook when someone hits a mark, but after that, they just go back to living the same life as everyone else, dealing with the same small annoyances, bouts of loneliness, and awkward conversations. No one escapes the ups and downs of life, and that's okay. We are all on the same level in this respect.

You're young, so you know that young people are subtly told every day that they are not enough. This message isn't as obvious as having the evil headmistress Agatha Trunchbull from Roald Dahl's *Matilda* yelling in your face. Instead, it's woven into sweet stories about kids with hidden talents who are underestimated and then turn out to be extraordinary. The thinking goes that since everyone is special in some way, one day you will discover your special talent or ability. If it's not evident now, it must be hidden and will reveal itself with the right opportunities. While this may be true, it also implies that the way you are now is not enough.

By focusing on what you could be—how amazing, world-changing, and mind-blowing you could be—writers like me sometimes are highlighting what you are not. The take-home message? You are not enough as you are and must upgrade to a version that is "better." To count in this world, you must bring greatness to it. Otherwise, you will become a nameless, faceless life with little to say for itself. Sound harsh? It is. And sadly, it is making many young people just like you want to check out from life entirely.

I am not an advocate for pressuring youth to change themselves. Society tends to see things in simple black-and-white terms, like equating failure at something in particular with being "worthless" because of it. If we fail to shoot a basketball through a hoop or we don't achieve a top mark on a mathematics quiz, it's easy to begin feeling like we're just like the rest of the "losers" out there.

But here's the truth—my professional opinion: You are enough just as you are. In fact, more than enough. You don't need to be extraordinary to be valuable or to lead a fulfilling, happy life. It's okay to be average. It's okay to shoot baskets and miss and do Sudoku puzzles and leave spaces blank. Those things are fun. In adulthood, a lot of leisure time is spent without "quizzes." Life is not a test. Life is just time and space, and an opportunity to have experiences.

Focus on what makes you happy, what you enjoy, and what makes you feel alive. That's where you'll find your true worth. If you stop keeping score, you'll be free to enjoy things more. The idea of "be great or go home" needlessly raises the stakes for even trying something new. It implies, "You can do it, but only if you are good at it right from the get-go. If not, you will be exposed as inadequate."

Can you see how you are being sent two contradictory (crazy making) messages? First, you are told you can do anything you set your mind to. Second, you are warned that you had better be great at whatever you set your mind to, or else doing it will be pointless.

My response? "Well, since you put it that way, I can't wait to take a crack at it!" NOT.

Under these constraints, most of us don't even try. The winner's circle isn't for us, and we know it. We aren't great now, so we never can be.

Which, of course, is complete nonsense.

The question you ask following any failure should be, "What now?" Do you give up, believing you just don't have it in you to be good or great at something? Or do you recognize your efforts for what they are— just "attempts," the starting point for everything you do in life? From crawling to walking, talking to asking someone out on a date, every fully developed skill or ability you have started with an attempt. And most of the time, you will fail. You will stumble, fall, stutter, turn back, or freeze in your tracks. You need to. Because all of it is important and necessary.

Charting Your Path Into the Future

You've probably been told you need to "think about your future." You may hear things like, "You think your boss is going to put up with that kind of behavior?" or "When you get to college, you'll need to do this for yourself." Or maybe, "Wait until you have to pay rent! I bet you'll have a little more appreciation for money then."

How could you not start to think about your future self and your place in the world given remarks like these?

It also should come as no surprise to anyone, given your age and stage in life, if you are thinking a lot about the different ways people support themselves and make money. Daydreaming is how you start to weigh your options, consider what's important to you, and think about if you can pursue a job doing work that is valuable and you enjoy.

As you start thinking about the future, questions about adulthood naturally come up. When do you actually become an adult? You and your parents might struggle to pinpoint the exact age or moment when you transition from being a teen to being an adult. Concepts like *responsibility* and *independence* are often used to define adulthood, but these terms can be vague and subjective. There isn't a clear definition of what it means to be an *adult*.

Markers of adulthood vary greatly. For some, it means being able to drink alcohol, drive a car, stay home alone, or have a job. It might also involve being responsible for someone else, like taking care of a younger sibling or having a pet. For others, adulthood might mean being married, having children, owning a home, or earning a degree from a four-year university. Some believe you've only truly become an adult when you have a job that carries social respect or importance, like being a doctor, lawyer, or entrepreneur.

Moving into adulthood brings a lot with it—things like getting and keeping a job, living independently, finding a relationship, and creating a social life. Given how much you have to juggle to make this transition, sometimes you might feel like you are just putting on a show of confidence, because deep inside, you are scared to death. If so, it's normal. It is also normal not to know, to change your mind, and to say you know what you are doing even when you don't. How could you not feel tempted to put on a brave face to stop people from judging you in today's world with all its pressure to have everything all figured out?

From celebrity culture to #goals to billionaires in their twenties, the expectation of perfection is all around us. Cultural messages often tell young people like you that they should be founding "unicorn" startups in their dorm rooms or at least living their best lives. Thus, it could feel like there's no viable alternative. Unless you're starting an industry-disrupting company, directing films, or launching a viral app, you might begin to feel like a failure by the age of eighteen.

But here's the reality: most of that pressure is just noise. It's okay to feel uncertain and take time to explore.

You are in the middle of a kind of awakening. This awakening brings with it a period of disorientation and questioning. You may feel overwhelmed by the hypocrisy, duplicity, and ulterior motives that seem to drive our world. Questions like "Who is really in charge?" and "How long will these issues go on?" become more pressing all the time. It is an important time to engage in questioning. Questions will be crucial for you to develop a deeper understanding of the world, and the role you want to play to shape it.

Young people are uniquely positioned as catalysts for change. Youth often have the clarity to see the disparities between what is said and what is done, and the inconsistencies in social norms and practices. While members of older generations may become desensitized or accustomed to longstanding problems, younger people bring fresh perspectives and are unburdened by the status quo. Having a fresh perspective is vital for recognizing and addressing issues that seem invisible because they have become normalized for those who have lived with them longer.

As each generation encounters distinct societal and techno-logical changes, new experiences and worldviews emerge that previous generations might not have encountered or understood.

Please remember, the journey of self-discovery and growth is a lifelong adventure. Stay true to yourself, seek out supportive allies, and face each challenge with the courage of your Five Champions. Your journey is just beginning, the world awaits you.

ACKNOWLEDGMENTS

A huge thank you to my fearless, smart, and focused editor, Stephanie Gunning, for helping me find my direction.

I appreciate my wife, Robin, for her unwavering support, belief in me, and constant encouragement—you keep me going.

Also, I must acknowledge my gratitude for:

- My good friend Don Kilburg, Ph.D., who gave me the push I needed to get started on this particular writing journey.
- Mary Ann McCabe, Ph.D., for being my champion in countless ways.
- Katheryn Grant, Ph.D., who taught me to trust the value of my ideas without taking myself too seriously and holding back.
- Sheldon Cotler, Ph.D., George Michel, Ph.D., and Sheila Ribordy, Ph.D., who believed in and took a chance on me.
- My Monday Night Men's Group, whose members keep teaching me how to put fun and joy into my life.
- And finally, to Erik Vysoky, Ph.D. —I am eternally indebted to you for saving my family. I miss our lunches at Mort's Deli under the elevated train on Wabash Avenue.

I am deeply grateful for the generations of thought leaders in psychology who paved the way for this work. The Five Champions in this book draw on archetypes explored by influential thinkers like Carl Jung, Joseph Campbell, and Robert Moore and Douglas

Gillette in their book *King, Warrior, Magician, Lover*. While these archetypes have inspired numerous frameworks, this book uniquely adapts them for teens, blending neuroscience and cognitive-behavioral strategies to tackle the challenges of modern adolescence. I hope this book has added to the conversation and helped move things forward, even in a small way.

RESOURCES

Website: www.drbrianrazzino.net

TikTok: @bitesized_therapy

Inquiries for speaking engagements: dr.brianrazzino@gmail.com

ABOUT THE AUTHOR

BRIAN E. RAZZINO, PH.D., is a licensed clinical psychologist with a private practice in Falls Church, Virginia. He received his doctorate in clinical psychology from DePaul University, and interned at Children's National Medical Center. He has served on the faculty of George Washington University and CNMC. He is a member of the American Psychological Association, the Virginia Academy of Psychology, and the Northern Virginia Academy of Clinical Psychologists. Dr. Razzino has worked with countless families on depression, anxiety, learning differences, and ADHD. He also has extensive clinical experience with complex developmental difficulties and training in neuropsychology. He is most proud of being a father and husband while doing what is closest to his heart, working with children and families.